Guns, Crime, and the Second Amendment

CRIME, JUSTICE, AND PUNISHMENT

Guns, Crime, and the Second Amendment

Justin Fernandez

Austin Sarat, GENERAL EDITOR

CHELSEA HOUSE PUBLISHERS
Philadelphia

Chelsea House Publishers

Editor in Chief Sally Cheney
Director of Production Kim Shinners
Production Manager Pamela Loos
Art Director Sara Davis
Senior Editor John Ziff
Production Editor Diann Grasse
Cover Design Keith Trego

Layout by 21st Century Publishing and
Communications, Inc., New York, N.Y.

First Printing

1 3 5 7 9 8 6 4 2

The Chelsea House World Wide Web address is
http://www.chelseahouse.com

Library of Congress Cataloging-in-Publication Data
CIP applied for ISBN 0-7910-5765-8

Contents

CRIME, JUSTICE, AND PUNISHMENT

Fears and Fascinations:

An Introduction to
Crime, Justice, and Punishment

By Austin Sarat

We live with crime and images of crime all around us. Crime evokes in most of us a deep aversion, a feeling of profound vulnerability, but it also evokes an equally deep fascination. Today, in major American cities the fear of crime is a major fact of life, some would say a disproportionate response to the realities of crime. Yet the fear of crime is real, palpable in the quickened steps and furtive glances of people walking down darkened streets. At the same time, we eagerly follow crime stories on television and in movies. We watch with a "who done it" curiosity, eager to see the illicit deed done, the investigation undertaken, the miscreant brought to justice and given his just deserts. On the streets the presence of crime is a reminder of our own vulnerability and the precariousness of our taken-for-granted rights and freedoms. On television and in the movies the crime story gives us a chance to probe our own darker motives, to ask "Is there a criminal within?" as well as to feel the collective satisfaction of seeing justice done.

Fear and fascination, these two poles of our engagement with crime, are, of course, only part of the story. Crime is, after all, a major social and legal problem, not just an issue of our individual psychology. Politicians today use our fear of, and fascination with, crime for political advantage. How we respond to crime, as well as to the political uses of the crime issue, tells us a lot about who we are as a people as well as what we value and what we tolerate. Is our response compassionate or severe? Do we seek to understand or to punish, to enact an angry vengeance or to rehabilitate and welcome the criminal back into our midst? The CRIME, JUSTICE, AND PUNISHMENT series is designed to explore these themes, to ask why we are fearful and fascinated, to probe the meanings and motivations of crimes and criminals and of our responses to them, and, finally, to ask what we can learn about ourselves and the society in which we live by examining our responses to crime.

Crime is always a challenge to the prevailing normative order and a test of the values and commitments of law-abiding people. It is sometimes a Raskolnikov-like act of defiance, an assertion of the unwillingness of some to live according to the rules of conduct laid out by organized society. In this sense, crime marks the limits of the law and reminds us of law's all-too-regular failures. Yet sometimes there is more desperation than defiance in criminal acts; sometimes they signal a deep pathology or need in the criminal. To confront crime is thus also to come face-to-face with the reality of social difference, of class privilege and extreme deprivation, of race and racism, of children neglected, abandoned, or abused whose response is to enact on others what they have experienced themselves. And occasionally crime, or what is labeled a criminal act, represents a call for justice, an appeal to a higher moral order against the inadequacies of existing law.

Figuring out the meaning of crime and the motivations of criminals and whether crime arises from defiance, desperation, or the appeal for justice is never an easy task. The motivations and meanings of crime are as varied as are the persons who engage in criminal conduct. They are as mysterious as any of the mysteries of the human soul. Yet the desire to know the secrets of crime and the criminal is a strong one, for in that knowledge may lie one step on the road to protection, if not an assurance of one's own personal safety. Nonetheless, as strong as that desire may be, there is no available technology that can allow us to know the whys of crime with much confidence, let alone a scientific certainty. We can, however, capture something about crime by studying the defiance, desperation, and quest for justice that may be associated with it. Books in the CRIME, JUSTICE, AND PUNISHMENT series will take up that challenge. They tell stories of crime and criminals, some famous, most not, some glamorous and exciting, most mundane and commonplace.

This series will, in addition, take a sober look at American criminal justice, at the procedures through which we investigate crimes and identify criminals, at the institutions in which innocence or guilt is determined. In these procedures and institutions we confront the thrill of the chase as well as the challenge of protecting the rights of those who defy our laws. It is through the efficiency and dedication of law enforcement that we might capture the criminal; it is in the rare instances of their corruption or brutality that we feel perhaps our deepest betrayal. Police, prosecutors, defense lawyers, judges, and jurors administer criminal justice and in their daily actions give substance to the guarantees of the Bill of Rights. What is an adversarial system of justice? How does it work? Why do we have it? Books in the CRIME, JUSTICE, AND PUNISHMENT series will examine the thrill of the chase as we seek to capture the criminal. They will also reveal the drama and majesty of the criminal trial as well as the day-to-day reality of a criminal justice system in which trials are the exception and negotiated pleas of guilty are the rule.

When the trial is over or the plea has been entered, when we have separated the innocent from the guilty, the moment of punishment has arrived. The injunction to punish the guilty, to respond to pain inflicted by inflicting pain, is as old as civilization itself. "An eye for an eye and a tooth for a tooth" is a biblical reminder that punishment must measure pain for pain. But our response to the criminal must be better than and different from the crime itself. The biblical admonition, along with the constitutional prohibition of "cruel and unusual punishment," signals that we seek to punish justly and to be just not only in the determination of who can and should be punished, but in how we punish as well. But neither reminder tells us what to do with the wrongdoer. Do we rape the rapist, or burn the home of the arsonist? Surely justice and decency say no. But, if not, then how can and should we punish? In a world in which punishment is neither identical to the crime nor an automatic response to it, choices must be made and we must make them. Books in the CRIME, JUSTICE, AND PUNISHMENT series will examine those choices and the practices, and politics, of punishment. How do we punish and why do we punish as we do? What can we learn about the rationality and appropriateness of today's responses to crime by examining our past and its responses? What works? Is there, and can there be, a just measure of pain?

CRIME, JUSTICE, AND PUNISHMENT brings together books on some of the great themes of human social life. The books in this series capture our fear and fascination with crime and examine our responses to it. They remind us of the deadly seriousness of these subjects. They bring together themes in law, literature, and popular culture to challenge us to think again, to think anew, about subjects that go to the heart of who we are and how we can and will live together.

*   *   *   *   *

There is no more controversial issue in the arena of crime, justice, and punishment than the issue of gun control. Crime in the United States is often more violent than in other nations because of the prevalence of firearms. Yet responding to this situation is made much more problematic by the Second Amendment and its guarantee of a "right to bear arms."

Guns, Crime, and the Second Amendment examines the role of guns in crime and the barriers that the Second Amendment poses as we try to devise effective solutions to the crime problem. It is well researched, well written, and well argued. Justin Fernandez has fully engaged with the most important debates regarding the Second Amendment, rightly using the distinction between individualist and collectivist interpretations as a touchstone for his analysis. The book provides a wide variety of very interesting analyses, from the history of the Second Amendment to the current controversy surrounding efforts to sue gun manufacturers. It will be a real resource for scholars and students alike.

A WELL-REGULATED CONTROVERSY

Outside the Washington Hilton Hotel, under gray skies and a chill typical for an early spring day in the nation's capital, a small crowd gathered around President Ronald Reagan's parked motorcade. It was March 30, 1981. The new president had just finished his second month in office. Reaganomics, the fall of the Berlin Wall, and the end of the cold war—each part of Reagan's popular legacy as president—lay ahead. Inside, the president was finishing his speech to a large audience at the AFL-CIO convention. Cameramen positioned equipment behind the rope cordoning off the security zone where officers from

Secret Service agents and police subdue would-be presidential assassin John Hinckley Jr. while two members of President Reagan's entourage try to aid the critically wounded press secretary, James Brady. Police officer Thomas Delahanty, shot in the neck, lies at left. The Hinckley case touched off renewed debate over gun control and the Second Amendment.

13

the Secret Service and the District of Columbia police force roamed. A woman in the crowd yelled something as the president emerged with his entourage. Reagan, striding toward his car, smiled and gave a big wave in her direction. Cameras clicked and more onlookers shouted, trying to get the president's attention.

Suddenly someone in the crowd began firing a gun. Shots ricocheted off concrete and brick, causing momentary confusion for everyone but Secret Service agent Timothy McCarthy, who jumped in front of the president at the sound of the gun and took a bullet in the abdomen. The bullets fired at the president were "exploding head Devastators" designed to spread on impact into twisty shards to shred a maximum amount of flesh and create a massive injury.

Cameras kept rolling and bystanders ran, dove, or stood frozen in astonishment or fear. Reagan, hit in the left chest but still standing, was pushed inside the car and rushed to the hospital. On the sidewalk, critically wounded, lay the president's press secretary, James Brady, and police officer Thomas Delahanty. Brady had sustained a massive gunshot wound to the head; Delahanty had been shot in the neck.

Months before, in a pawnshop in Dallas, Texas, the shooter had filled out a federal form in order to purchase a handgun. John Hinckley Jr. hadn't been entirely truthful in filling out that form, but without any fact verification, a waiting period, or a detailed background check, the pawnshop owner had quickly sold him the gun.

Hinckley, who first bought a handgun in August 1979, soon built a small firearms collection. Meanwhile, he was apparently experiencing mental problems; he reportedly played Russian roulette in November and December of 1979. In 1980 Hinckley began taking prescription antidepressants and tranquilizers.

The object of Hinckley's obsession: actress Jodie Foster, in a scene from the motion picture Taxi Driver.

After seeing the movie *Taxi Driver*, in which Jodie Foster played a young prostitute, Hinckley became obsessed with the actress. When he read, in the May 1980 issue of *People* magazine, that Foster would be attending Yale University in the fall, Hinckley decided to enroll in a writing course at Yale. He left letters and poems in Foster's mailbox and called her twice, hoping to establish a relationship with the film star. To his dismay, however, no relationship developed.

Hinckley's obsession with Foster led to a more dangerous fixation. Like a character in *Taxi Driver*, he decided to assassinate a politician. Through this "historic deed," he would later write, he hoped to win Foster's "respect and love." Hinckley chose President Jimmy Carter as his target. For weeks he crisscrossed the country on the president's trail, but he never got the chance to shoot at Carter. Once, at an airport, security guards found guns in his bags. The weapons were confiscated and Hinckley had to pay a fine, but he was easily able to buy replacements for the firearms. In the November presidential election, Ronald Reagan defeated Carter.

On March 29, 1981, Hinckley checked into the Park Central Hotel in Washington, D.C. The following day he wrote Jodie Foster a letter informing her of his undying love and his plan to shoot the president. Then he took his handgun to the Washington Hilton and awaited Reagan's appearance.

The assassination attempt on Ronald Reagan marked the beginning of a new era in the interpretation of the Second Amendment of the United States Constitution, which reads:

> A well-regulated Militia, being necessary to the security of a free State, the right of the people to keep and bear Arms, shall not be infringed.

The essential question in the gun controversy is whether the Second Amendment provides an individual right to own or carry guns. Interpretations of the Second Amendment by scholars, commentators, and courts generally fall into one of two categories: individualist or collectivist.

Collectivists, mostly gun control advocates, oppose reading an individual right into the Second

Amendment. Attorney and law review author Roy G. Weatherup makes the case for the collectivist view as follows:

> Delegates to the Constitutional Convention had no intention of establishing any personal right to keep and bear arms. Therefore the "individualist" view of the Second Amendment must be rejected in favor of the "collectivist" interpretation, which is supported by history and a handful of Supreme Court decisions on the issue. . . . the nature of the Second Amendment does not provide a right that could be interpreted as being incorporated into the Fourteenth Amendment. It was designed solely to protect the states against the [federal] government, not to create a personal right which either state or federal authorities are bound to respect. The contemporary meaning of the Second Amendment is the same as it was at the time of its adoption. The federal government may regulate the National Guard, but may not disarm it against the will of state legislatures. Nothing in the Second Amendment, however, precludes Congress or the states from requiring licensing and registration of firearms; in fact, there is nothing to stop an outright congressional ban on private ownership of all handguns and all rifles.

Supporters of the "individualist" reading of the Second Amendment, mostly gun rights advocates, argue that an individual right to bear arms is explicitly granted in the Second Amendment, and fully supported by the history of gun rights in England and the American colonies, as well as the history of the actual drafting of the Bill of Rights. The history of the drafting of the Second Amendment shows that while an individual right for everyone to "bear Arms" was not inherited from the English common law—the law upon which most American law was patterned during colonial times—the right of self-defense was considered fundamental by the Framers of the Constitution, all of whom had lived through the experience of having a "well-regulated" militia

A scene from the French and Indian War, 1755. The Framers of the U.S. Constitution, living at a time when many people had to defend themselves from Native Americans or wild animals, seem to have believed in the right of individuals—and not just militia groups—to bear arms.

resist disarmament by the British. The Framers—living at a time when many people had to hunt wild animals for food, defend against armed attack by Native Americans, and survive in cities and towns that lacked police—appeared to believe that there was an individual right, derived from the need for self-defense and militia preparedness, to bear arms.

Individualists sometimes claim that the attempt to avoid an individualist reading of the Second Amendment is dishonest—that certain rights, including the grant of the right to bear arms, are at the mercy of a cultural elite whenever convenient. Robert Dowlut, an attorney for the National Rifle Association, observed:

> History teaches us the unfortunate lesson that cultural values supplant constitutional rights whenever the cultural elite consider a right too burdensome to suit the needs of the moment. The outlandish pronouncement in Dred Scott "that the Negro might justly and lawfully be reduced to slavery for his benefit," the shameful court-approved internment of Japanese-Americans during World War II, and the separate but equal doctrine that officially existed until 1954 are all examples of the evils that result when cultural values are given more weight than constitutional rights.

Dowlut also argues that "the Framers considered the right to keep and bear arms peculiarly important and also uniquely vulnerable to infringement," protecting individuals "against even popular conceptions of the public good."

Commentator Vernon Gray also believes that the gun prohibition movement intends to dishonestly discredit the Second Amendment in its applicability to individuals, weaken the concept and acceptability of self-defense, and "change our traditions as they relate to firearms."

Behind the debate over how to properly read and apply the Second Amendment lies genuine concern for the public good. Gun control advocates argue that too many people in a heavily armed society become victims to otherwise preventable gun violence. The statistics support the notion that gun violence is expensive, tragic, and often linked to the easy availability of weapons.

For example, the *Journal of Trauma* reported that taxpayers pay more than 80 percent of the medical costs for treatment of firearm-related injuries. According to the National Center for

Health Statistics, 14 children in the United States are killed each day by gun violence. A study by the Harvard School of Public Health found that 59 percent of all children in grades 6 to 12 knew where to get a gun if they wanted one, and two-thirds of those students claimed that they could acquire a firearm within 24 hours.

But the problem of gun violence as it relates to gun availability is complex. Statistics can be interpreted in different ways. Handgun availability is often a focus of gun control supporters who claim that the easy purchase of a handgun fuels crimes of passion, opportunity, and violence. According to the U.S. Justice Department, 78 percent of all murders of law enforcement officers involved handguns. From 1977 to 1996, according to the Bureau of Alcohol, Tobacco and Firearms, the U.S. firearm industry produced 39,024,786 handguns. But another 50 million rifles and shotguns were manufactured during the same period. While gun control legislation in the 1990s made it more difficult for people with criminal records to buy handguns from licensed gun shops, guns remain available from shows or private sales, including so-called swap-meets. This displeases gun control advocates who say that the easy availability of handguns and assault-style weapons leads to unnecessary deaths.

However, a mid-1980s survey of convicted felons in 12 state prisons found that fewer than 1 percent obtained guns at gun shows. A 1997 Justice Department survey put the figure at only 2 percent.

For some gun control supporters, even 2 percent is too much. But many criminologists believe that even fairly restrictive gun control legislation, including background checks at gun shows, wouldn't prevent such tragedies as the mass shootings at Columbine High School in Littleton, Colorado.

Gun rights advocates argue that depriving citizens of the right to bear arms leaves citizens more vulnerable to criminal attack. Citing statistics tending to show that citizens experience less violent crime in states where laws allow for the carrying of concealed firearms, gun rights advocates argue that attempts to disarm otherwise law-abiding citizens aren't good for public safety. Gun rights advocates also cite studies showing that guns are used about five times more often to stop crimes than to commit them.

Public opinion favors both sides of the gun control debate. Most voters continue to believe strongly that the Constitution protects the right of individuals to bear arms, including handguns, according to a *Washington Post*–ABC News poll published on September 9, 1999. But 63 percent of the public supports moderate gun control measures. The survey found suburban residents are as likely as urban residents to support a range of gun control measures. More than 8 of 10 surveyed supported the requirement that guns be sold with trigger locks and favored background checks at gun shows. In rural areas, such support is significantly lower. However, about two-thirds oppose a nationwide ban on the sale of handguns. And voters are evenly split on whether there should be a national ban on carrying concealed weapons.

The Hinckley assassination attempt permanently disabled James Brady, whose brain injuries were so severe that he was not expected to live through surgery, and Officer Delahanty, whose left-arm paralysis forced him to take early retirement from police work. Outraged at how easy it was for criminals and other high-risk individuals to obtain guns and ammunition, James Brady's wife and a group of citizens that included the survivors of other gun violence tragedies began lobbying for new legislation. In 1993, after years of acrimonious

With James Brady seated at his right, President Bill Clinton signs into law the Brady Act, November 30, 1993.

debate and intense pressure on Congress from both well-financed sides of the gun control issue, the legislation named after Sarah Brady's husband was passed by Congress and signed into law by President Bill Clinton.

Many gun rights advocates were outraged at the passage of the Brady Act. Gun control advocates, on the other hand, criticized loopholes in the bill and urged the adoption of stronger measures aimed at preventing the sale of guns to anyone with a history of criminality or mental instability.

The gun debate continues to escalate. While statistics showed a 21 percent drop in gun deaths from 1993 to 1997 and diminishing firearms injuries and gun crime since the passage of the Brady Act, gun violence is still much higher than it was in the 1960s. The United States remains the annual leader in gun violence. In 1995, for example, handguns were used to kill 2 people in New Zealand, 15 in Japan, 30 in Great Britain, 106 in Canada, 213 in Germany, and 9,390 in the United States. Fully 232 years earlier, a Massachusetts patriot had worried about such gun violence but still stated in a newspaper article his firm belief in an individual right to bear arms.

THE HISTORY OF THE RIGHT TO BEAR ARMS

John Adams, the future second president of the United States, wrote in the *Boston Gazette* in 1763, "Resistance to sudden violence, for the preservation not only of my person, my limbs, and life, but of my property, is an indisputable right of nature which I have never surrendered to the public by the compact of society, and which perhaps, I could not surrender if I would."

Under the common law of England, there was no universal right to "bear arms," but everyone had a right of self-defense. In addition, many citizens were expected to keep guns for militia preparedness; in England during most of the millennium before the American Revolution, there was a universal *duty*

Minutemen fire at retreating British soldiers during the Battle of Concord, April 19, 1775. The American colonists had chafed at British attempts to disarm them in the years leading up to the Revolutionary War.

25

among men to take up arms in defense of the country. Most commentators agree, however, that during the bulk of England's history, no right existed to keep weapons for peacekeeping or self-defense, although most citizens viewed any attempt at disarmament to be a corrupt and unlawful practice of the government.

For hundreds of years before the 1066 Norman invasion, a general obligation existed for every person to keep weapons handy for the potential defense of England. The obligation to defend England in a citizen army dates from as early as A.D. 690. The concept that all subjects were potentially soldiers with the responsibility to maintain their own weaponry was established during the reign of King Alfred from 871 to 901.

As early as 1181, the right to bear arms, in the service of the king, was first made explicitly mandatory in the Assize of Arms issued by King Henry II. In 1215, King John was forced to sign the Magna Carta (Great Charter), ancestor to the constitutions of state and federal government in modern America. The Magna Carta's 63 articles set forth restrictions on the king's power over lands and people and described authority vested in the people to exercise power, not merely to be free from certain evils of authority. The introductory article of the Magna Carta states, "Ye have also granted to all the free men of Our kingdom, for Us and Our heirs forever, all the liberties underwritten." Although the Magna Carta identified fundamental rights, these rights were empowered inconsistently in England through the time of the American Revolution. The right to bear arms was never once made a universal right for all Englishmen, despite the ancient understanding that the defense of England required a citizen army.

In 1328, before the first firearms were widely available, Parliament passed the Statute of Northhampton, which provided that carrying a weapon was an indictable offense. Another English statute, the Game Act—passed some 343 years later in 1671—provided

King John seals the Magna Carta, 1215. The ancestor of America's state and federal constitutions, the Magna Carta delineated fundamental rights of English citizens. The right to bear arms was not among those fundamental rights.

that no person who did not own lands "of the yearly value of £100 other than the son and heir of an esquire or other person of higher degree" should be allowed to keep guns, making possession of a firearm illegal and allowing the confiscation of illegally owned guns. For a short time a few years earlier, gunsmiths were required to report on weekly gun manufacture and sales, firearm imports were banned, and anyone judged dangerous to the kingdom was ordered disarmed.

Militias became well regarded by the English, who for centuries witnessed the victories of England's armies of free men over larger and professional forces of other countries. The English also endured religious and political power struggles between the Crown and the Parliament that illustrated the necessity of having some right to resist government tyranny. When James I asserted that Parliament existed only by "the grace and permission of our ancestors and us," the House of Commons passed the Protestation of December 18, 1621, which asserted:

> That the Liberties, Franchises, Privileges and Jurisdictions of Parliament, are the ancient and undoubted birthright and inheritance of the subjects of England; and that the arduous and urgent affairs concerning the King, State and defence of the realm, and of the Church of England, and the making and maintenance of laws, and redress of [mischief] and grievances, which daily happen within this realm, are proper subjects and matter of counsel and debate in Parliament: and that . . . every member of the House hath, and of right ought to have, Freedom of Speech, to propound, treat, reason and bring to conclusion the same.

The king responded by walking into the House of Commons and tearing the page containing the Protestation from the Journal.

The beginning of the rule of law in England emerged from this power struggle. Parliament and English lawyers prevailed in asserting the view that the king's prerogative is only what the law allows. Courts of common law asserted jurisdiction to inquire into the legality of acts by the monarchy.

Yet after the rise of the common law to its predominant position of authority, English kings continued to abuse their power by illegally trying to disarm portions of the populace. Charles I used the military to abuse the power of the Crown by imposing martial law, imprisoning men without trial, and forcing loans. These acts angered the English and led to the drafting of a petition of rights in Parliament that Charles I was forced to agree to and sign. The petition, an assertion of the power of Parliament and the common law, contained a long list of grievances.

But England was to lurch backward to pre–Magna Carta days again. The king secretly consulted his judges, who assured him that his signature would not be binding. Soon afterward, in 1629, the king dissolved Parliament and began the long period of personal rule that ended in the Great Rebellion and the execution of the king.

The ecclesiastical canons of 1640 emphatically affirmed the theory of the Divine Right of Kings and, in addition, promulgated the doctrine of nonresistance that made bearing arms against the king tantamount to bearing arms against God. The doctrine of "non-resistance" played an important role in religion and politics in both England and America through the time of the American Revolution.

Statutes passed in 1661 and 1662 declared that the king had the sole right of command and disposition of the English militia and its organization. However, in practice, it was the landowners who controlled the means of raising a militia for the country's defense. Meanwhile, foreign wars required England to maintain a standing army that, with the consent of Parliament, exceeded 16,000 men by the end of the reign of Charles II. English country gentlemen became more secure in their control of the militia with the passing of the Game Act in 1671 forbidding gun ownership to commoners without sufficient landholdings.

A little more than 100 years before the drafting of the Second Amendment, the protection of the liberties of the English was committed entirely to Parliament and the landowners, preventing the creation of a citizen army. Militia preparedness, not an individualist right to bear arms, was still relied upon for England's defense.

Once James II began systematically enlarging the standing army and seeking repeal of Parliamentary power and reinstatement of the prerogative of kings to act without regard to the common law, England again faced a crisis that led to a revolt and overthrow of a king. Before James II fled to France in exile, he had asked Parliament to abandon its reliance on the militia in favor of standing armies, arguing that the militia was "not sufficient" for putting down internal rebellions and that a standing army "in constant pay" was required for defense against aggression outside and within the country. Parliament refused, and King James II sought victory in a lawsuit to achieve his aim of restoring the absolute sovereignty of English kings over English laws.

The success at chasing James II from the throne led to the passage of a statute, known as the Bill of Rights, that declared the "ancient rights and liberties" of the realm and addressed the problem of the relationship of a king to the armed forces. The English Bill of Rights allowed the king to have an army only with the express consent of Parliament and forbade the king to disarm or dismantle the militias.

There was no recognition of any personal right to bear arms in England on the part of subjects generally, but the new law protected the right to bear arms for those qualified individuals under the common law who were allowed to have guns in the first place. Eventually, Parliament deprived the people entirely of the right to bear arms in parts of Scotland. The English common law was not used to challenge the power of Parliament to disarm certain portions of the populace.

Charters granted by the king established the governments of the American colonies. An important feature of this arrangement was a provision securing for the inhabitants of the colonies the rights of Englishmen born and living in England. But from the beginning, the restriction of gun ownership to landed gentlemen in England did not transfer to America, and neither did much else pertaining to the practice of bearing arms. All freemen in the colonies were allowed to keep and bear arms in self-defense from attacks from Native Americans and wild animals. There is no historical debate on this issue. Although the common law of England was the common law of the American colonies, the law shaped, but did not determine, how Americans applied English precedent in colonial courts.

The legal relationship of Great Britain and the American colonies became more than an academic problem after the end of the French and Indian War in 1763. The cost of the war was enormous, and the British government decided that the colonies should share it. In his efforts to tax and govern the colonies, King George III acted in two capacities: as a king armed with the prerogatives of his office, and as an agent of the British Parliament, which at that time was under his personal control.

The British in the 1760s noted that the New England "province" consisted of more than 150,000 well-armed militiamen who were mostly highly accurate marksmen. King George III was concerned that the colonists, if they remained armed, would present a threat to his law enforcement authority. With the growing disagreement between the colonists and the British over such things as taxes and criminal justice, the king decided that an unarmed American colony would be far easier and cheaper to rule.

In 1774, the English Parliament banned the importation of firearms (long guns and pistols) and ammunition into the colonies, and authorized British searches of persons, property, and private or commercial shipments of goods. The British governor in Massachusetts, John Gage, directed the effort to enforce the search and seizure laws in Boston. British authorities and troops seized whatever weapons were found, and then further enraged the New England colonists by turning the weapons over to the British military instead of preserving the confiscated arms for eventual return to their owners as originally promised. Efforts by various individuals to get the governor to release confiscated weapons, as private property, mostly failed.

Massachusetts patriot Josiah Quincy believed that in being asked by the British to surrender their weapons, the colonists were being asked to give up fundamental rights.

Local patriots such as Samuel Adams, James Otis, Josiah Quincy, and John Adams, and commentators in England such as Edmund Burke, led the effort to remind the colonists that in being asked to surrender their weapons, the colonists were being persuaded by the British to give up fundamental rights.

In the years following the 1770 Boston Massacre, and before England resorted to the weapons and ammunition import ban in 1774, colonists often responded to the English attempt at disarmament by handing over defective weapons and hiding good ones. The colonists hoarded the short-barreled, shotgun-like blunderbusses; the long-distance and highly accurate American-manufactured Pennsylvania rifles; the Brown Bess, a bayoneted British military-issue rifle often stolen or purchased by the colonists; and other muskets, carbines, fowling pieces, and pistols in good condition.

Shortly before the first skirmishes of the Revolution at Concord, Massachusetts, in 1775, local colonists—teenagers and old men, tradesmen and professionals, farmers and merchants—drew upon a stockpile of ammunition and weapons from dozens of local farms. The "shot heard 'round the world" was fired largely because the British sought to prevent such a shot from ever being fired, and the colonists resisted disarmament.

The "compact of society" John Adams referred to in the Boston newspaper, some 12 years before the battles of Lexington and Concord, is the same social contract that provided philosophical support and authority for protecting the fundamental rights of Americans from British government encroachment. According to author Henry St. George Tucker, the right to possess weapons was one of the "protections or barriers [that] have been erected which serve to maintain inviolate the three primary rights of personal security, personal liberty, and private property." Tucker's analysis echoed that of famed English jurist William Blackstone, and many other commentators and experts in the colonies and Great Britain.

Blackstone believed that the right to carry a weapon was an important right but was not as unlimited as the right to self-preservation. In his famous 1765 book *Commentaries on the Laws of England*, Blackstone noted that that the right of British subjects "of having arms for their defence, suitable to their condition and degree, and such as are allowed by law . . . is indeed a public allowance, under due restrictions, of the natural right of resistance and self-preservation, when the sanctions of society and laws are found insufficient to restrain the violence of oppression."

The colonists had acknowledged the authority of the king, but only in accordance with their charters and with the same restrictions that limited his power in Britain. Unwilling to accept inferior status, most colonists could not admit the authority of Crown and Parliament to bind them "in all cases whatsoever" and fell back on the doctrine of fundamental law as expressed in 1764 by James Otis:

> 'Tis hoped it will not be considered as a new doctrine, that even the authority of the Parliament of [England] is circumscribed by certain bounds, which if exceeded their acts become those of mere power without right, and consequently void. The judges of England have declared in favour of these sentiments, when they expressly declare; that acts of Parliament against natural equity are void. That acts against the fundamental principles of the British constitution are void. This doctrine is agreeable to the law of nature and nations, and to the divine dictates of natural and revealed religion.

This concept of fundamental law was based upon English legal tradition. The Americans improved upon English law where they could, and there is little doubt that the right to foster better self-defense by maintaining arms for self-defense became understood as a fundamental right throughout much of colonial America before the American Revolution.

After the Revolutionary War, the challenge for the Founding Fathers was to create a system sufficiently empowering the individual against government tyranny or corruption. The healthy distrust of all government— particularly one with the power or custom of raising and maintaining a standing army in peacetime—led to the drafting and inclusion of the Second Amendment in the Bill of Rights.

A potential flaw in the collectivist argument comes from George Washington's opinion of militias as being useless in comparison to a standing army. The armies of the American Revolution were numerous—at least 14 in number—with 13 colonial militias also involved—and the debate over the relative merits of each continued during the fighting. Washington wrote to the Continental Congress in September of 1776 as follows:

> To place any dependence upon Militia, is, assuredly, resting upon a broken staff. Men just dragged from the tender Scenes of [domestic] life; unaccustomed to the din of Arms; totally unacquainted with every kind of military skill, which being followed by a want of confidence in themselves, when opposed to Troops regularly [trained], disciplined, and appointed, superior in knowledge and superior in Arms, makes them timid, and ready to fly from their own shadows. . . . The Jealousies of a standing Army, and the Evils to be apprehended from one, are remote; and, in my judgment, situated and circumstanced as we are, not at all to be dreaded . . . if I was called upon to declare upon Oath, whether the Militia have been most serviceable or hurtful upon the whole; I should subscribe to the latter.

Given the importance of Washington's opinions to the statesmen who drafted the Constitution, the militia clause of the Second Amendment could not have been inspired solely by notions of adequate defense of the new country by militias. Given the long-standing English practice of restricting a right to bear arms to certain classes of people, and given the English experience with tyranny—and the Americans' recent experience with Great Britain's export of tyranny—the Second Amendment represented a statement against disarmament, whatever the practical results would be.

Article II of the Articles of Confederation, the first (and ultimately unsuccessful) constitution of the newly independent United States, provided that each state would retain "its sovereignty, freedom, and independence" and that "every state shall always keep up a

A fistfight between a Massachusetts government supporter and a member of Shays' Rebellion. The 1786–87 uprising by discontented farmers helped convince leaders of the states that a federal Constitution was needed.

well-regulated and disciplined militia, sufficiently armed and accoutred." The maintenance of a state militia was clearly not for the purposes of opposing or defending against the new American government. However, the new American government appeared to need some protection from the people. The government was unable to pay Revolutionary War veterans back pay and promised pensions from the war. The veterans, under the name of the Society of Cincinnati, organized a peaceful march on the capital, Philadelphia, in the summer of 1783.

The ex-soldiers threatened violence and the seizure of Congress. The Congress adjourned, its members sufficiently alarmed to flee to Trenton, New Jersey. The soldiers eventually gave up their efforts, and the officers who led them escaped punishment. In 1786, another citizen revolt broke out. Shays' Rebellion saw Massachusetts farmers oppressed by debt attack a federal arsenal and fight several skirmishes with the state militia before finally being routed in February 1787. Under the Articles of Confederation, Congress had been unable to help Massachusetts put down the rebellion. This, and other evidence of weakness in the national government, prompted leaders of the states to gather in Philadelphia during the summer of 1787 to draft a new federal constitution.

THE FOUNDATION OF AMERICAN GOVERNMENT

THE DRAFTING OF THE SECOND AMENDMENT

On September 17, 1787, delegates to the Constitutional Convention signed the Constitution. Before it became the law of the land, however, nine states would have to ratify, or approve, the document. Opponents of ratification, called Anti-Federalists, objected that the Constitution gave the federal government too much power, and the people too little. Largely in response to these objections, Congress drafted 12 amendments, of which 10—the Bill of Rights we know today—would ultimately be adopted.

During the state conventions for the ratification of the U.S. Constitution, delegates often turned to their state constitutions for guidance in determining

The signing of the U.S. Constitution, September 17, 1787. In order to ensure ratification by the states, the Framers committed to a Bill of Rights. Among the 10 amendments that make up the Bill of Rights is the Second Amendment, which deals with the "right to bear Arms."

the final language of portions of the Bill of Rights, and in particular the final language of the Second Amendment. A minority faction in the Pennsylvania ratification convention was the first to make proposals for a Bill of Rights. Among the 15 proposals submitted on December 13, 1787—the day after the Constitution was ratified 46-23 at the Pennsylvania convention—the seventh proposal, which ensured a right to bear arms, showed the influence of Pennsylvania's state constitution. Pennsylvania's constitution read, in pertinent part: "the people have a right to bear arms for the defence of themselves and the state; and as standing armies in the time of peace are dangerous to liberty, they ought not to be kept up; and that the military should be kept under strict subordination to and governed by the civil power."

The seventh proposal by the Pennsylvania Minority provided that: "the people have a right to bear arms for the defence of themselves and their own State, or the United States, or for the purpose of killing game; and no law shall be passed for disarming the people or any of them, unless for crimes committed, or real danger of public injury from individuals; and as standing armies in the time of peace are dangerous to liberty, they ought not to be kept up; and that the military shall be kept under strict subordination to and be governed by the civil power."

The fundamental ideas proposed by the Pennsylvania Minority, and by a similar minority in Massachusetts, eventually found their way into the final draft of the Bill of Rights and became the First, Second, Fourth, Fifth, Sixth, Eighth, and Tenth Amendments.

The Anti-Federalist Pennsylvania Minority, in a writing entitled "The Address and Reasons of Dissent of the Minority of the Convention of Pennsylvania to their Constituents," published in the *Pennsylvania Packet and Daily Advertiser* on December 18, 1787, identified how the new American government through a standing army or by government-directed militias would tyrannize a citizenry that lacked, among other rights, the right to bear arms:

> [I]t appears that the Congress under this constitution will not possess the confidence of the people, which is an essential requisite in a good government; for unless the laws command the confidence and respect of the great body of the people, so as to induce them to support them . . . they must be executed by the aid of a numerous standing army, which would be inconsistent with every idea of liberty; for the same force that may be employed to compel obedience to good laws, might and probably would be used to wrest from the people their constitutional liberties. The Framers . . . appear to have been aware of this great deficiency; to have been sensible that no dependence could be placed on the people for their support: but on the contrary, that the government must be executed by force. They have therefore made a provision for this purpose in a permanent STANDING ARMY, and a MILITIA. . . . A standing army in the hands of a government placed so independent of the people, may be made a fatal instrument to overturn the public liberties; it may be employed to enforce the collection of the most oppressive taxes, and to carry into execution the most arbitrary measures. An ambitious man [with] the army at his devotion, may step up into the throne, and seize upon absolute power. The absolute unqualified command that Congress have over the militia may be made instrumental to the destruction of all liberty, both public and private; whether of a personal, civil or religious nature. . . . the personal liberty of every man probably from sixteen to sixty years of age, may be destroyed by the power Congress have in organizing and governing [the militia]. . . . the absolute command of Congress over the militia may be destructive of public liberty; for under the guidance of an arbitrary government, they may be made the unwilling instruments of tyranny. The militia of Pennsylvania may be

marched to New England or Virginia to quell an insurrection occasioned by the most galling oppression, and aided by the standing army, they will no doubt be successful. . . . Thus may the militia be made the instruments of crushing the last efforts of expiring liberty, of riveting the chains of despotism on their fellow citizens, and on one another. This power can be exercised not only without violating the constitution, but in strict conformity with it.

When James Madison, the author of the Second Amendment, proposed the Bill of Rights to Congress in 1789, he wrote that the amendments concerning the press and arms "relate first to private rights." After Madison's proposal, Federalist leader Tench Coxe wrote of what became the Second Amendment: "Civil rulers . . . may attempt to tyrannize, and as the military forces which must be occasionally raised to defend our country, might pervert their power to the injury of their fellow-citizens, the people are confirmed by the next article in their right to keep and bear their private arms."

Madison endorsed Coxe's analysis, which was reprinted without contradiction. In fact, the draft that became the Second Amendment was seen as embodying the sentiment of Samuel Adams, who proposed in the Massachusetts ratifying convention in 1789 a bill of rights affirming: "That the said Constitution be never construed to authorize Congress to . . . prevent the people of the United States, who are peaceable citizens, from keeping their own arms."

Anti-Federalist George Mason, largely responsible for the Virginia Bill of Rights, spoke as follows at the Virginia convention to ratify the federal Constitution: "There are various ways of destroying the militia. A standing army may be perpetually established in their stead. I abominate and detest the idea of government, where there is a standing army. The militia may be here destroyed by that

James Madison, the author of the Second Amendment, believed that the people should be "confirmed . . . in their right to keep and bear their private arms" as a safeguard against government tyranny.

method which has been [practiced] in other parts of the world before; that is, by rendering them useless—by disarming them."

Discourse regarding the controversy over the right to bear arms was not limited to the state ratifying conventions. A contemporaneous article in the *Federal Gazette & Philadelphia Evening Post* contradicts modern claims that the Framers never intended to guarantee the private ownership of arms: "As civil rulers, not having their duty to the people duly before them, may attempt to tyrannize, and as the military forces which must be occasionally raised to defend our country, might pervert their power to the injury of their fellow citizens, the people are confirmed by the next article in their right to keep and bear their private arms."

Another article, published on January 29, 1788, and authored by James Madison under the name Publius, extols the advantage of protecting the right to bear arms, lauds a broad-based militia, and scorns governments that do not trust people with arms. "Besides the advantage of being armed," Madison wrote, "which the Americans possess over the people of almost every other nation, the existence of subordinate governments to which the people are attached, and by which the militia officers are appointed, forms a barrier against the [enterprises] of ambition, more insurmountable than any which a simple government of any form can admit of. Notwithstanding the military establishments in the several kingdoms of Europe, which are carried as far as the public resources will bear, the governments are afraid to trust the people with arms."

Madison believed in private ownership of arms and distrusted governments that did not protect such a right, reasoning that: (1) members of the military can be armed without a constitutional right to keep and bear arms, as "in the several kingdoms of Europe"; (2) the militia should be broad-based and subject to some state control; and (3) only despotic governments are afraid to trust the people with arms.

Just as revealing as Madison's opinions, the Constitutional Convention rejected proposals that did not guarantee a right to keep and bear arms. So did the early Congress. For example, a motion in the Senate to insert "for the common defence" after the words "bear arms" was defeated on September 9, 1789.

Self-defense was considered a natural and common law right, and it was found in a number of state constitutions. At the New Hampshire convention, the first convention to meet to decide whether to ratify the Constitution, the delegates recommended that the Constitution include a bill of rights and a provision that "Congress shall never disarm any citizen, unless such as are or have been in actual rebellion." North Carolina's Constitution guaranteed that "the people have a right to bear arms, for the defence of the State." The North Carolina Supreme Court later construed this right to mean that "[f]or any lawful purpose—either of business or amusement—the citizen is at perfect liberty to carry his gun." North Carolina and Rhode Island refused to ratify the Constitution until individual rights, including the right to bear arms, were recognized by amendments.

Virginia's convention deemed the right to keep and bear arms necessary to its proposed Bill of Rights. Virginians in the convention debates focused on the individual nature of the right to arms, as opposed to simply demanding that the states be allowed to have a militia. Anti-Federalist Patrick Henry asserted, "The object is, that every man be armed. . . . Every one who is able may have a gun."

The Framers mostly understood that the Second Amendment encompassed the right to keep and bear arms for personal defense. Reflecting this understanding, the Ninth Circuit Court of Appeals recently opined that "[t]he Second Amendment embodies the right to defend oneself and one's home against physical attack."

The Framers were also aware of the dangers involved with a broad right to bear arms. Pennsylvania's minority proposal reserved the explicit power

"Everyone who is able may have a gun," firebrand Patrick Henry declared at Virginia's ratification convention.

to disarm people for "crimes committed" and in instances where there was "real danger of public injury from individuals." Massachusetts's minority proposal on arms would have restricted this right to "peaceable citizens." New Hampshire's majority proposal on arms reserved the explicit power to disarm those who "are or have been in actual rebellion." Such explicit police powers as these, however, were not adopted because the Framers probably felt that such powers were unnecessary, that the constitutional right would not apply to well-accepted prohibitions against criminal misconduct. Many of the Framers and their contemporary commentators acknowledged that the right to "bear Arms" was not universal—that criminals and other potentially dangerous or undeserving persons were not entitled to be armed as a matter of fundamental right.

Legislative history demonstrates that the Framers clearly recognized that in addition to the importance of a militia to the security of a free state, a guarantee preserving an individual right to keep and to bear arms was also important. The Framers refused to adopt proposals that omitted or limited such an individual guarantee. In comments on the final form of the Second Amendment, historian Joyce Lee Malcolm wrote that the Second Amendment was "meant to accomplish two separate goals crucial to the maintenance of liberty . . . to guarantee the individual's right to have arms for self defense" and to preserve the militia tradition. Malcolm believed that the Second Amendment mention of the importance of a well-regulated militia "was not intended to limit ownership of arms to militia members" or to "return control of militia to the states but rather to express the preference for a militia over a standing army."

In the first reported opinion interpreting the Second Amendment, the Georgia Supreme Court considered the right to bear arms so fundamental that, despite the absence of a guaranteed right to bear arms in Georgia's constitution, the court extended the Second Amendment to apply to the state, using the following reasoning to void a statute forbidding the sale, keeping, or having about the person a pistol, "save such pistols as are known and used as horseman's pistols":

> It is true, that these adjudications are all made on clauses in the State Constitutions; but these instruments confer no new rights on the people which did not belong to them before. . . . The language of the Second Amendment is broad enough to embrace both Federal and State Governments nor is there anything in its terms which restricts its meaning. . . . [D]oes it follow that because the people refused to delegate to the general government the power to take from them the right to keep and bear arms, that they designed to rest it in the State governments? Is this a right reserved to the States or to themselves? Is it not an unalienable right, which lies at the bottom of every free government? We do not believe that, because the people withheld this arbitrary power of disfranchisement from Congress, they ever intended to confer it on the local legislatures. . . . The right of the whole people, old and young, men, women and boys, and not militia only, to keep and bear arms of every description, and not such merely as are used by the militia, shall not be infringed, curtailed, or broken in upon, in the smallest degree; and all this for the important end to be attained: the rearing up and qualifying a well-regulated militia, so vitally necessary to the security of a free State.

Although this decision contravened the United States Supreme Court's holding that the Bill of Rights restrains only the national government, many agreed with the Georgia Supreme Court's position, and eventually this view prevailed in the language of the Fourteenth Amendment.

Law school professor Eugene Volokh convincingly argues that the way the Second Amendment and militia preamble was written—similar to provisions in other state constitutions—does not weaken the "right to keep and bear Arms." For example, a "free speech preamble" in the 1842 Rhode Island Constitution— "[t]he liberty of the press being essential to the security

of freedom in a state, any person may publish senti-
ments on any subject, being responsible for the abuse
of that liberty"—does not mean that the right to free
speech is limited to instances where the exercise of
free speech is "essential to the security" of the state.
As Professor Volokh points out, state constitutions
contain numerous examples of this kind of writing.

Such wording in other constitutions shows that
the Second Amendment was a fairly commonplace
construction and not a rare or oddly written passage.
This provides further support to the argument that a
right does not expire when courts conclude that the
justification given for the right is no longer valid or
is no longer served by the right, or that a right exists
only when, in a court's judgment, the right furthers
the goals identified in its justification clause.

A Militia By Any Other Name

The he gun control debate focuses upon the way the militia clause—"A well-regulated Militia, being necessary to the security of a free State"—might limit the "right of the people to keep and bear Arms" to militia-related gun ownership. Understanding the meaning of "free State" is important. The colonists believed that in a free state, government does what the people want it to do.

In June 1776, Virginia became the first state to create a constitution and Bill of Rights. Section 13 of the Virginia Bill of Rights provided that "a well-regulated militia composed of the body of people, trained to arms, is the proper, natural, and safe

Michigan Militia founder Norman Olson. Though their political views are often far to the right of the mainstream, members of the modern militia movement may actually fulfill a function the Framers envisioned for armed citizens: deterring government infringement on personal liberties.

defense of a free state." Section 13 became the basis for all subsequent militia provisions and the Second Amendment.

Documents from the time of the drafting of the state and federal constitutions indicate that the term *militia* referred to all of the people, or at least all of those treated as full citizens of the community. In pamphlets entitled *Letters from the Federal Farmer to the Republican,* an important writer, thought to be Richard Henry Lee, referred to a "militia, when properly formed, [as] in fact the people themselves." The Federal Farmer criticized the new Constitution's absence of a Bill of Rights and wrote that "to preserve liberty, it is essential that the whole body of the people always possess arms, and be taught alike, especially when young, how to use them."

George Mason, responsible for drafting the Virginia Bill of Rights, defined the term *militia* accordingly: "I ask, Who are the militia? They consist now of the whole people, except a few public officers." The Anti-Federalists, including George Mason, in arguing for the inclusion of the Second Amendment in the Bill of Rights, considered the state militia to be an effective counterbalance to the power of a standing army. But the Anti-Federalists did not like the degree of federal government power over the militia, and they argued that the Constitution left the arming of the state militia exclusively to the federal government. During the Virginia debates over the ratification of the federal Constitution, Patrick Henry expressed this concern in asking, "When this power is given to Congress without limits or boundary, how will your militia be armed?" The right of keeping and bearing of arms in a "well-regulated Militia" of the states was understood as a "right of the people" not dependent on the whim of the federal government.

The militia historically, as the Framers knew of

VIRGINIA BILL of RIGHTS

DRAWN ORIGINALLY BY GEORGE MASON AND
ADOPTED BY THE CONVENTION OF DELEGATES

June 12, 1776.

A Declaration of Rights made by the Reprefentatives of the good People of Virginia, affembled in full and free Convention; which Rights do pertain to them, and their Pofterity, as the Bafis and Foundation of Government.

I.

That all Men are by Nature equally free and independent, and have certain inherent Rights, of which, when they enter into a State of Society, they cannot, by any Compact, deprive or diveft their Pofterity; namely, the Enjoyment of Life and Liberty, with the Means of acquiring and poffeffing Property, and purfuing and obtaining Happinefs and Safety.

II.

That all Power is vefted in, and confequently derived from, the People; that Magiftrates are their Truftees and Servants, and at all Times amenable to them.

III.

That Government is, or ought to be, inftituted for the common Benefit, Protection, and Security, of the People, Nation, or Community; of all the various Modes and Forms of Government that is beft, which is capable of producing the greateft Degree of Happinefs and Safety, and is moft effectually fecured againft the Danger of Mal-adminiftration; and that, whenever any Government fhall be found inadequate or contrary to thefe Purpofes, a Majority of the Community hath an indubitable, unalienable, and indefeafible Right, to reform, alter, or abolifh it, in fuch Manner as fhall be judged moft conducive to the public Weal.

IV.

That no Man, or Set of Men, are entitled to exclufive or feparate Emoluments or Privileges from the Community, but in Confideration of public Services; which, not being defcendible, neither ought the Offices of Magiftrate, Legiflator, or Judge, to be hereditary.

V.

That the legiflative and executive Powers of the State fhould be feparate and diftinct from the Judicative; and, that the Members of the two firft may be reftrained from Oppreffion, by feeling and participating the Burthens of the People, they fhould, at fixed Periods, be reduced to a private Station, return into that Body from which they were originally taken, and the Vacancies be fupplied by frequent, certain, and regular Elections, in which all, or any Part of the former Members, to be again eligible, or ineligible, as the Laws fhall direct.

That

Section 13 of the Virginia Bill of Rights, enacted in June 1776, provided that "a well-regulated militia composed of the body of people, trained to arms, is the proper, natural, and safe defense of a free state." That section became the basis for all subsequent militia provisions and the Second Amendment.

it, was a 13-century-old Anglo-Saxon institution. Composed of all subjects or citizens capable of bearing arms, including minors, the militia represented a duty of personal service to protect and defend the government in a time of need. Obligation, not volunteerism, was at the militia system's core for most of its history in England. Militia members in England were typically required to render service to the king in proportion to the member's status as landowner. An obligation to serve went with the land for tenants. In the colonies, however, the land ownership aspects of England's militia system were not copied. It also appears that in addition to the aspect of duty involved in militia service, the Framers set out to ensure more than a constitutionally recognized duty for militia service in the Second Amendment: the option to keep arms to fight against any source of tyranny.

The American Constitution was drafted to provide that Congress shall have power to call forth the militia "to execute the laws of the Union, suppress insurrection, and repel invasions." Congress was also authorized to "provide for organizing, arming, and disciplining the militia, and for governing such part of them as may be employed in the service of the United States; reserving to the States respectively the appointment of the officers, and the authority of training the militia according to the discipline prescribed by Congress."

The Constitution also provided that "[t]he President shall be Commander-in-Chief of the Army and Navy of the United States, and of the militia of the several States, when called into the actual service of the United States." If duty was the extent of the Framers' concern, the Second Amendment was not necessary to invoke the obligatory service role of militia preparedness, since Congress was given the power to "call forth" the militia mentioned in the federal Constitution. Like the militia in England, the American militia as defined in the Constitution occupied a specific service role to the head of the government and was not meant to defend against the government itself.

The Framers, familiar with hundreds of years of England's internal struggles against corrupt standing armies, tyrannical kings, and attempts at disarmament, drafted the Second Amendment to improve upon the English militia tradition as a means of ensuring that militia preparedness could never be compromised by the disarming of all law-abiding individuals. A proper militia, to the Framers' way of thinking, was a self-regulated militia. Although the usual role of any English or American militia would be in service of the head of government, in the national defense, the militia of England and the colonies existed as self-regulating forces with self-defense of the people—the free state—as their main purpose.

Gun control supporters often argue that there is no longer a need for the kind of militia the Framers had in mind. However, as recently as World War II, Americans witnessed a useful role for the kind of "grass-roots" militia preparedness the Framers appeared to use as their basis for drafting the Second Amendment. While the National Guard, created by the National Defense Act of 1916, was deployed overseas and along the coastlines of America during World War II, militias of the kind the Framers envisioned, such as the "Maryland Minutemen," took part in preparing to defend against perceived invasion threats to U.S. soil. Nazi submarine warfare in the Atlantic and the Japanese invasion of the Aleutian Islands made it seem possible to many that "ordinary" Americans—those not serving abroad in the military or National Guard—might have to take up arms in the same manner as the farmers of Lexington and Concord nearly two centuries earlier. (In England, ordinary nonmilitary subjects in the countryside near the English Channel prepared to meet Nazi invaders with baskets of pepper and pitchforks because firearms were in short supply.) The explicit foreign self-defense purpose of the Second Amendment remains viable so long as there are citizens at home during wars fought overseas. As the threat to American soil during World War II illustrates, there is no way to predict whether a citizen militia will ever be needed to supplement military and paramilitary organizations run by national or state governments. Without an individual right to bear arms existing in the Second Amendment, the national defense purpose of militias—which the Framers intended the Second Amendment to preserve—cannot be fulfilled.

Some gun control advocates who seek to avoid an individual rights reading of the Second Amendment argue that the right to bear arms pertains solely to "well-regulated" militias and that "well-regulated" only involves regulation by state government. In Article I, Section 8, the Constitution provides that the federal government can use militias to "execute the laws of the union, suppress insurrections and repel invasions." Today, the U.S. Code defines a militia as consisting of "all able-bodied males at least 17 years of age and, except as provided in section 313 of title 32, under 45 years of age who are, or who have made a declaration of intention to become, citizens of the United States and of female citizens of the United States who are members of the National Guard." The U.S. Code lists the classes of militia as being: (1) the organized militia, which consists of the National Guard and the Naval Militia; and (2) the unorganized militia, which consists of the members of the militia who are not members of the National Guard or the Naval Militia. Organized militias like the modern National Guard or the compulsory militias existed in America between 1792 and 1901 in every state. Each required government financial support.

Some American colonies maintained militias as highly systematic organizations for a century or more before the American Revolution. These organizations were hierarchical and adhered to codes determining membership, training, officer selection, punishment for rule violations, and method of mobilization. The militia

In Federalist Paper No. 29, Alexander Hamilton argued that in America, a well-regulated militia was not one that was highly trained in the manner of a professional military force.

clause of the Second Amendment cannot be read to exclude militias that are not regulated by the state—or at least, that does not seem to have been the understanding of the Framers of the Constitution.

In Federalist Paper No. 29, Alexander Hamilton argued that a well-regulated militia in America was not one that was highly trained in the manner of a professional military force. "The project of disciplining all the militia of the United States," Hamilton wrote,

> is as futile as it would be injurious if it were capable of being carried into execution. A tolerable expertness in military movements is a business that requires time and practice. It is not a day, nor a week nor even a month, that will suffice for the attainment of it. To oblige the great body of the yeomanry and of the other classes of the citizens to be under arms for the purpose of going through military exercises and evolutions, as often as might be necessary to acquire the degree of perfection which would entitle them to the character of a well-regulated militia, would be a real grievance to the people and a serious public inconvenience and loss.

A well-regulated militia could in theory be controlled by citizens with arms as opposed to being controlled by a government entity. Indeed, it is very doubtful that the Framers would have thought that unarmed citizens could trust the government to provide them with enough weapons quickly enough whenever the need for a militia arose. So even if the Framers never intended to have a Second Amendment militia defend against the members' own government, they did not trust the government's ability to run the kind of "well-regulated" militia they knew from experience helped preserve liberty. To read the Second Amendment as allowing ownership and possession of weapons only when an individual belongs to a government-regulated militia is not only to ignore history and the Framers' intent but to completely miss the point of why the Second Amendment was thought necessary and vital, as were the other protections in the Bill of Rights against government power, corruption, and tyranny.

Recently, the Supreme Court has stated that the militia is composed of "civilians primarily" and that "all citizens capable of bearing arms constitute the reserved military force or reserve militia of the United States." In a dissenting opinion in 1990, Justice William Brennan

In a 1990 opinion, Supreme Court justice William Brennan wrote that the Framers "designed the Bill of Rights to prohibit our Government from infringing rights and liberties presumed to be pre-existing."

noted that rights are not "given to the people from the government" and that the "Framers of the Bill of Rights did not purport to 'create' rights"; rather, "they designed the Bill of Rights to prohibit our Government from infringing rights and liberties presumed to be pre-existing." Under Brennan's thesis, the Second Amendment could not possibly represent a fundamental right for individuals and be solely applicable to the government regulation of a militia.

In *Commentaries on the Constitution*, Joseph Story, an associate justice of the U.S. Supreme Court from 1811 to 1845, emphasized the importance of the Second Amendment. He described the militia as the "natural defence of a free country" not only "against sudden foreign invasions" and "domestic insurrections," but also against "domestic usurpations of power by rulers." Story wrote that "the right of the citizens to keep and bear arms" is properly considered "as the palladium of the liberties of a republic; since it offers a strong moral check against the usurpation and arbitrary power by rulers; and will generally, even if these are successful in the first instance, enable the people to resist and triumph over them."

Judge Thomas Cooley, one of the most influential constitutional commentators of the 19th century, noted that the state might call into its official militia only "a small number" of the eligible citizenry. Cooley wrote that if the right to keep and bear arms "were limited to those enrolled, the purpose of this guaranty might be defeated altogether by the action or neglect to act of the government it was meant to hold in check."

Theodore Schroeder, one of the most important developers of the theory of freedom of speech early in this century, remarked that "the obvious import" of the Second Amendment "is to promote a state of pre-paredness for self-defense even against the invasions of government, because only governments have ever disarmed any considerable class of people as a means toward their enslavement."

Like other commentators, Schroeder would con-sider it a "privilege and immunity" of citizenship (a constitutional right of all citizens) to keep arms that could be employed to fight tyranny—even tyranny from the state or federal government. Ironi-cally, this argument is also strongly made in remarks by Chief Justice Roger Taney in the infamous case of *Dred Scott v. Sandford*, which the Supreme Court decided in 1857. Taney suggested that citizenship included the right to possess arms. During slavery, it was of course inconceivable that slaves would be allowed weapons, and under no reading of the Constitution were slaves to enjoy constitutional rights or rights as citizens. But in the *Dred Scott* decision the Court went a bit further, declaring that no black person—slave or free—could be an American citizen "in the sense in which the word citizen is used in the Constitution of the United States." The tyranny of the state and federal government in maintaining the institution of slavery would qualify as a legitimate reason to revolt—or to form militias to resist the imposition of slavery.

The Second Amendment clearly embodies the notion that the people of the United States are free to fight attempts to remove their liberty. Slaves could not be considered citizens without also recognizing that, as citizens, the slaves had a Second Amendment right to bear arms—and a strong reason to use the threat of violence as a means to obtain their liberty. A narrow reading of the Second Amendment results in the inescapable conclusion that modern citizens have no right to resist potential enslavement by government— however remote such a possibility seems—by keeping, and if necessary by bearing, arms.

Similarly, the purpose of the Second Amendment extended recognition to an individual's right to engage in armed self-defense against criminal conduct. Slavery, now almost universally considered criminal conduct, is again a good point of reference for understanding why the Second Amendment has to pertain to individual gun ownership rights. Yet the debate continues despite so much historical evidence and the fact that even the Framers did not believe that every person was eligible to bear arms.

THE COURTS ON THE RIGHT TO BEAR ARMS

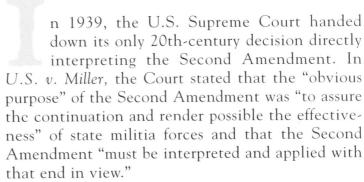

I n 1939, the U.S. Supreme Court handed down its only 20th-century decision directly interpreting the Second Amendment. In *U.S. v. Miller,* the Court stated that the "obvious purpose" of the Second Amendment was "to assure the continuation and render possible the effectiveness" of state militia forces and that the Second Amendment "must be interpreted and applied with that end in view."

Gun control advocates often cite *Miller* as support, arguing that the Second Amendment was created only to prevent the federal government from disarming a state militia, and that Congress can disarm any or all individuals because the Second Amendment provides

The Supreme Court's decisions on the meaning of the Second Amendment have been relatively few and, some legal commentators believe, somewhat confusing.

no individual right to either carry or own a gun. It is true that courts have constantly rejected the individual rights position of gun rights advocates. In 1994, the American Bar Association's Task Force on Gun Violence recommended that the leaders of the legal profession educate the public and lawmakers regarding the meaning of the Second Amendment to "make widely known the fact that the United States Supreme Court and lower federal courts have consistently, uniformly held that the Second Amendment to the United States Constitution right to bear arms is related to 'a well-regulated militia' and that there are no federal constitutional decisions which preclude regulation of firearms in private hands." The ABA's position on the Second Amendment reveals a belief that the first portion of the Second Amendment, the militia clause, controls the rest of the Second Amendment's meaning, obliterating the individual right so many gun advocates insist American history and the original intent of the Framers support without question.

The ABA's Second Amendment position through the 1990s included the notion that "[f]ederal and state court decisions in this century have been uniform in the view that the Second Amendment permits the exercise of broad power to limit private access to firearms by all levels of government" and that *Miller* held that "the scope of the people's right to bear arms is qualified by the introductory phrase of the Second Amendment regarding the necessity of a 'well-regulated militia' for the 'security of a free State.'"

Some commentators feel, however, that there is no other Supreme Court decision in our nation's history that has been more distorted and cluttered by misinformation than *Miller*, and that the lower federal courts have consistently misinterpreted the Supreme Court's holding in *Miller*. According to some legal scholars, there has been a collective judicial assumption made about the Second Amendment that the Framers could not have really meant that individuals should have a judicially enforceable right to keep and bear arms.

Frequently, lower courts dispose of Second Amendment claims by applying a "*Miller* test." The courts do not seem to agree about what the *Miller* test is, however, and use *Miller* to overcome a carefully crafted claim in several ways. Courts can conclude that *Miller* directs the granting of Second Amendment protection only where there is some demonstrable relationship between the weapon, which is restricted, and the maintenance of a militia. As it became evident that almost any type of weapon was potentially effective in combat or as a means of self-defense preparedness, courts shifted the focus to the state of mind of the possessor and asked whether the person using or possessing the weapon had first and foremost in mind an intent to ensure the maintenance and efficacy of a militia. When a plaintiff could overcome these arguments, the court could play a "*Miller* trump card" by finding that no individual can make such a colorable (legitimate) Second Amendment claim because the Second Amendment protects only a collective right of state citizens (as a group) to form militias and to employ them to oppose federal tyranny. The court can also vary this theme and read the Second Amendment as protecting only the states' right to maintain militias free from federal control.

The *Miller* case reached the Supreme Court on appeal from a Kansas district court opinion holding that a section of the National Firearms Act violated the Second Amendment. The defendants, Jack Miller and Frank Layton, were charged with unlawfully transporting certain firearms in interstate commerce. The trial court judge sustained a demurrer (an allegation that the facts are true but the law does not provide a basis for requiring the defendants to answer or defend against the charges). The demurrer alleged that the section of the National Firearms Act that the defendants were accused of violating itself violated the Second Amendment.

The Supreme Court reversed this decision and remanded, or returned, the case to the district court. Remarkably, the defendants in *Miller* disappeared after the district court ruled in their favor.

The case made it to the Supreme Court because the government appealed the decision of the district court. The district court's initial opinion in *Miller* disproves claims made by courts and critics of the Second Amendment that federal courts have uniformly rejected challenges to federal regulation of firearms on Second Amendment grounds. Justice McReynolds, for a unanimous Supreme Court, held in *Miller* simply that:

> [i]n the absence of any evidence tending to show that possession or use of a "shotgun having a barrel of less than eighteen inches in length" at this time has some reasonable relationship to the preservation or efficiency of a well-regulated militia, we cannot say that the Second Amendment guarantees the right to keep and bear such an instrument. Certainly it is not within judicial notice that this weapon is any part of the ordinary military equipment or that its use could contribute to the common defense.

The Supreme Court's decision in *Miller* was limited; there wasn't any searching inquiry into the origin and development of the Second Amendment. Arguing for the government, Solicitor General Robert Jackson had presented a "collective-rights" interpretation of the Second Amendment. (No oral argument presented the opposing viewpoint because the defendants had not retained defense counsel.) Although McReynolds's opinion in *Miller* assumes some connection between militias and the right to keep and bear arms, had the Court accepted the government's collective-rights argument, the case would have likely been decided on the issue of standing (whether the defendant had proper reason and status to be in court) because the defendants were not members of any militia. Under the

Justice James C. McReynolds wrote the Supreme Court's 1939 U.S. v. Miller *opinion, whose precise significance lower courts have since found elusive.*

government's reading of the Second Amendment, the Court should have found that Jack Miller had no standing to invoke the Second Amendment in the district court. However, the justices did not explore the consequences of the Court's own finding that history showed "plainly enough that the Militia comprised all males physically capable of acting in concert for the common defense. . . . these men were expected to appear bearing arms supplied by themselves and of the kind in common use at the time."

Justice McReynolds described the purpose of the

Second Amendment as giving assurance to the Constitution and "rendering possible the effectiveness" of the militia. McReynolds noted further that "the debates in the Convention, the history and legislation of Colonies and States, and the writings" of commentators all show "plainly enough that the Militia comprised all males physically capable of acting in concert for the common defense."

This emphasis on the common defense does not foreclose the right of individual self-defense. Arguably, the common defense is merely self-defense in the aggregate. Had the defendants in *Miller* retained an attorney for oral argument, and had the attorney cited evidence about the militia and weapons that militia members generally possessed or correctly argued that the introductory phrase of the Second Amendment merely expressed a widespread sentiment against standing armies and was not meant to qualify or to limit an individual right to keep or bear arms, the result might have been far different. Even if *Miller* is someday overruled by the Supreme Court, courts have held that the Second Amendment does not apply to the states. Although courts over the past 50 years have found that most of the Bill of Rights applies to the states, the Second Amendment's applicability to state governments awaits further litigation.

United States v. Cruikshank, an old Reconstruction-era case, remains as a barrier. *Cruikshank* originated in Louisiana with a 16-count indictment against more than 100 individuals alleging, under the Enforcement Act of 1870, that the defendants conspired to "hinder and prevent" two African-American citizens from exercising certain "rights and privileges." Among the rights and privileges asserted were the "lawful right and privilege to peaceably assemble together with each other and with other citizens of the United States for a peaceable and lawful purpose" and the right of "bearing arms for a lawful purpose."

The Court's holding in *Cruikshank* emphasized that the guarantees in the Bill of Rights operate to restrain governments as opposed to individuals. *In dicta* (judicial writing that is not usually considered important enough to create judicial precedent affecting future cases), however, the Court recited the then-current doctrine that the Bill of Rights did not apply to the states, and it is this portion of the opinion upon which modern lower courts tend to rely. In dismissing the First Amendment count, the Supreme Court in *Cruikshank* found that despite the passage of the Fourteenth Amendment, the First Amendment "was not intended to limit the powers of the State governments in respect to their own citizens, but to operate on the National government alone." The Court reasoned that because the right of the people to peaceably assemble was neither "created" by the Constitution nor "was its continuance guaranteed, except as against congressional interference," the people must look to the states for protection of this right. The Court relied on similar reasoning in dismissing the Second Amendment claim, noting that "bearing arms for a lawful purpose" was "not a right granted by the Constitution" and holding that the Second Amendment's language "means no more than it shall not be infringed by Congress."

Strangely, lower courts continued to cite *Cruikshank* for the proposition that the Second Amendment poses no obstacle to state gun control legislation even if the result turned out to be an outright ban on certain kinds of weapons. While lower courts must apply Supreme Court precedent as it exists, every other constitutional provision except for the Second Amendment has been found to apply to state governments through the incorporation of the Fourteenth Amendment.

One purpose of the Fourteenth Amendment was

to empower the former slaves whose protections under the Bill of Rights were rendered useless by the *Dred Scott* decision. Although Jim Crow—laws providing for "separate but equal" treatment of blacks and whites—would interfere with the empowerment of African Americans under the Fourteenth Amendment until the sixth decade of the 20th century, the Fourteenth Amendment mandated privileges and immunities, due process of law, and equal protection for citizens. Senator Jacob Howard concluded that the Fourteenth Amendment protected the right to keep and bear arms and that "[t]he great object of the first section of this amendment is, therefore, to restrain the power of the States and compel them at all times to respect these great fundamental guarantees."

Following the adoption of the Fourteenth Amendment, the right to keep and bear arms for personal security was also included in an act commonly called the Freedmen's Bureau Act, which was enacted after Congress overrode a veto by President Andrew Johnson. The act provided that the right to have full and equal benefit of all laws "including the constitutional right to bear arms, shall be secured to and enjoyed by all citizens of such State or district without respect to race or color, or previous condition of slavery."

Only one other Supreme Court case, *Presser v. Illinois*, addressed in any detail the applicability of the Second Amendment to the states. *Presser* involved an Illinois statute that made it a crime to "associate as a military company, or organization, or to drill or parade with arms" in Illinois without a license from the governor, who had unlimited authority to revoke any license. Exceptions were recognized by law for the military and the Illinois militia. In September of 1879, Presser and 400 fellow members of a society calling itself Lehr und Wehr

Verein marched without a license in the streets of Chicago. Presser, convicted and fined $10, complained that the Illinois law had the effect of depriving him of his Second Amendment right to keep and bear arms. The Court answered that the right to gather as a group and hold armed parades was not included in the right to keep and bear arms and that "the amendment is a limitation only upon the power of Congress and the National government, and not upon that of the States." The Court cited *Cruikshank* for support of this proposition. *In dicta*, the justices suggested that to the extent that state citizens are also members of the national militia, state regulation that prohibited "the people from keeping and bearing arms, so as to deprive the United States of their rightful resource for maintaining the public security" would not be sustainable, "even laying the [Second Amendment] out of view." This suggests that the state's right to restrict the lawful bearing of arms is not absolute even when the Second Amendment is not considered.

The first lower court cases interpreting *Miller* appeared during World War II. In 1942, a First Circuit decision created much of the subsequent confusion over *Miller*. *Cases v. United States* was one of the very few lower court cases to carefully parse the language of *Miller*. The *Cases* court rejected the logic of *Miller*. Looking instead to the state of mind of the person claiming a Second Amendment right, the court found that a person must have in mind the maintenance or preservation of the militia as a paramount concern before being able to prevail on a Second Amendment claim. In rejecting the *Miller* test, the court stated that if it were to take the reasoning in *Miller* to its logical conclusion, the federal government could ignore the Second Amendment and limit the keeping and bearing of arms by a single individual as well as by a group of individuals, but it cannot prohibit the possession or use of any weapon that has any reasonable relationship to the preservation or efficiency of a well-regulated militia. The *Cases* court was of the opinion that the Supreme Court in *Miller* was not formulating a general rule applicable to all cases, and commented that the *Miller* ruling, "if intended to be comprehensive and complete would seem to be already outdated, in spite of the fact that it was formulated only three and a half years ago, because of the well known fact that in the so called 'Commando Units' some sort of military use seems to have been found for almost any modern lethal weapon."

The court concluded that following the *Miller* rule would tend to make the limitation of the Second Amendment absolute, and prevent the government from prohibiting "the possession or use by private persons not present or prospective members of any military unit, of distinctly military arms, such as machine guns, trench mortars, anti-tank, or anti-aircraft guns." In abandoning any attempt "to formulate any general test by which to determine the limits imposed by the Second Amendment" the court addressed the facts in the record and found that the armed defendant was "transporting and using the firearm and ammunition purely and simply on a frolic of his own and without any thought or intention of contributing to the efficiency of the well-regulated militia that the Second Amendment was designed to foster as necessary to the security of a free state." The court found that there was no conflict between the federal statute and the Second Amendment and upheld the conviction.

Far from reading it as rendering no protection to an individual's right to keep and bear arms, the *Cases* court reasoned that the *Miller* opinion, if intended as a general rule, afforded entirely too much protection to a wide range of potentially destructive devices that

Oakland police officers examine a variety of legal and illegal weapons turned over by citizens in a gun swap. In the Cases v. United States decision, the First Circuit Court of Appeals rejected the logic of the Supreme Court's Miller decision, stating that it would prohibit the government from banning the possession of any weapon useful to a militia—which would be nearly any weapon.

individuals might seek to possess. The court thus created a state of mind requirement to the Second Amendment where none had previously existed.

The court in *United States v. Tot* offered questionably one-sided historical analyses of the Second Amendment to support its reading of *Miller*. The defendant in *Tot* was convicted of violating a federal law that prohibited the possession of a firearm capable of being fitted with a silencer. One of the grounds upon which the defendant attacked his conviction was the Second Amendment. The *Tot* court, like the *Cases* court, thought that *Miller* left a good deal unanswered, and made a sweeping conclusion in remarking that "it is abundantly clear" that the Second Amendment "unlike those providing protection of free speech and freedom of religion was not adopted with individual rights in mind but as a protection for the States in the maintenance of their militia organizations" against possible encroachment by the federal government. The court also concluded that the colonists "wanted no repetition of that experience in their newly formed government," implying that the Framers drafted the amendment as a mere constitutional guideline to remind the federal government not to become worse than what it replaced, and not as an individual right.

Yet judicial refusal to recognize an individual right as an absolute right does not necessarily mean that the individual right does not exist. The history of rights in general suggests that the Framers intended the Bill of Rights not as a grant of rights but as a recognition of rights the people already had and were entitled to keep. No court has yet adequately supported with a fair reading of history and the drafting of the Second Amendment the *Tot* court's argument that the Second Amendment "was not adopted with individual rights in mind."

Most federal court decisions following challenges to post-1968 federal gun control legislation seek support not from historical documents but from conclusions traceable to the *Cases* and *Tot* precedents. The individual right has been dismissed in courts with statements such as "There is no absolute constitutional right of an individual to possess a firearm." While this statement is absolutely accurate in the context of the fact that not every colonist was deemed worthy or capable of owning a gun, the statement has been taken out of context and used as a basis to suggest that there is no individual right at all to own a gun.

As with any individual right, the government may impose limitations based upon certain criteria usually involving conflicts with other rights. This can be done without declaring that the individual right does not exist. When a district court in Pennsylvania observed that the Second Amendment "is not a bar to Congressional regulation of use and possession of firearms," the court was proposing the right outcome without providing the right rationale. The reason Congress can regulate (not bar) the use and possession of firearms is not that no individual right exists to use or bear arms, but simply that all individual rights can be regulated in some fashion depending upon circumstances. Not even the staunchest Anti-Federalist would have claimed that there is an absolute right against the federal government's power to regulate guns.

Courts and commentators who argue against an absolute Second Amendment right are debating against a "straw man," a weak argument advanced simply so that it can be demolished. No scholar has ever argued that the Second Amendment right is any more absolute than the First Amendment rights. Such willingness to make arguments against illusory opposition demonstrates the lower courts' reluctance to discuss even in theory situations under *Miller* where government regulation of firearms would infringe upon the protections given by the Second Amendment. The result is a lack of guidance for legislators and plaintiffs alike.

Similar to the *Tot* court's reasoning, a district court judge in *United States v. Jones* reasoned that since there is no absolute constitutional right of an individual to possess a firearm, "the test of determining the constitutionality" (of the federal statute in question) "depends on finding a rational basis for the particular classification." Under this judge's formulation, no right that is not absolute can qualify as "fundamental." Fundamental rights invoke the highest scrutiny of federal courts. Under the test in *Jones,* not a single right in the Constitution would qualify as fundamental because none would be absolute.

The judicial record is devoid of any similar statements being made about the freedom of speech or religion. The result is that the Second Amendment alone is treated as if it did not contain any right at all. This view has been expressly given by lower federal courts that have cited *Miller* as showing that historically, "the right to keep and bear arms is not a right given by the United States Constitution." A New Hampshire district court following *Miller* stated that it is well established that the Second Amendment is not a right but "a limitation upon the power of Congress and the national government." No language in *Miller* suggests such findings. No explanations for how the Second Amendment limits the power of Congress accompany the court's assertions.

Following the lower court decisions in *Cases* and *Tot,* there was almost no Second Amendment litigation until after the federal gun control legislation of the late 1960s found challengers. At first, the challenges were defeated in court according to the *Cases* "state of mind" requirement or the *Tot* "collective theory" interpretation. But once these challenges were overcome by strong lawyering, the courts simply changed the rules.

In the case of *United States v. Warin*, the court inaccurately maintained that Second Amendment jurisprudence since *Miller* had precisely followed the language and meaning of *Miller*. In *Warin*, the defendant was convicted by an Ohio district court for possessing an unlicensed submachine gun in violation of federal law. Warin appealed on the grounds that he was a member of the "sedentary militia" of Ohio and that he had been making improvements to the weapon in question so that he might offer it "to the Government as an improvement on the military weapons presently in use." In affirming Warin's conviction, the court found that *Miller* articulated no clear rule. The *Warin* court cited its earlier decision in *Stevens v. United States* for additional support. The *Stevens* Court cited *Miller* for the proposition that there can be "no serious claim to any express constitutional right of an individual to possess a firearm" and that the Second Amendment applies only "to the right of the State to maintain a militia." The *Warin* court then concluded that the Second Amendment clearly "guarantees a collective rather than an individual right" and provided insight into its concerns by commenting: "[The *Cases* court] noted the development of new weaponry during the early years of World War II and concluded that it was not the intention of the Supreme Court to hold that the Second Amendment prohibits Congress from regulating any weapons except antiques 'such as a flintlock musket or a matchlock harquebus. . . .' If the logical extension of the defendant's argument for the holding of Miller was inconceivable in

"[I]t was not the intention of the Supreme Court to hold that the Second Amendment prohibits Congress from regulating any weapons except antiques 'such as a flintlock musket or a matchlock harquebus,' " a lower court maintained in the United States v. Warin *decision, which affirmed the conviction of a man charged with possession of an unlicensed submachine gun.*

1942, it is completely irrational in this time of nuclear weapons."

Of course, no one was arguing about any right to keep or bear nuclear weapons in *Warin*, and the *Warin* court was not faced with an argument that Congress lacked all power of arms regulation by operation of the Second Amendment.

In *United States v. Hale*, the Eighth Circuit described *Cases* as "one of the most illuminating circuit opinions on the subject of 'military' weapons and the Second Amendment" and based its opinion in large part on *Cases* and not *Miller*. *Hale* involved the prosecution and conviction of an individual for possession of unregistered machine guns in violation of federal law. The defendant appealed his conviction, arguing that the indictment violated his Second Amendment rights, and that based on *Miller* he had every right to possess the machine guns because they were just the sort of weapons that would be employed by a military unit, and thus were weapons that would contribute to the preservation or efficiency of the militia.

The Eight Circuit rejected this interpretation of *Miller*, claiming without explanation that the Supreme Court's language in *Miller* was merely recognizing "historical residue." The Eight Circuit Court cited *Cases* for the proposition that to obtain Second Amendment protection, a claimant must prove that weapon possession was reasonably related to a well-regulated militia. "Where such a claimant presented no evidence either that he was a member of a military organization or that his use of the weapon was 'in preparation for a military career,' " the court said, "the Second Amendment did not protect the possession of that weapon."

The *Hale* court thus conditioned Second Amendment rights upon a showing of membership in, or preparation for membership in, a military organization without discussing what level of activity was required for such preparation. The *Hale* decision could be read differently and overruled using its own rationale if "preparation for a military career" was interpreted properly as the very few behaviors required for preparation for militia activity—there being no such thing as a "militia career" to the way of thinking of probably every colonist and Framer. Those behaviors could have been merely having one's weapon hanging by the door or even obtaining access to a weapon by knowing, like some of the Minutemen of Lexington and Concord, the secret farmhouse locations of the stockpiles.

To the Framers, "militia" meant quite the opposite of an organized military organization. To lower courts in the modern era, however, "militia" seems to mean anything that will avoid a finding in favor of an individual right from the Second Amendment.

And when defining militia is not useful, the courts have relied on the questionable pedigree of *Cruikshank* and *Presser*.

In upholding a city's ban on the possession of handguns within city limits, the federal court in *Quilici v. Morton Grove* stated that the Second Amendment had not been applied to the states through the Fourteenth Amendment, and thus was ineffective as a restraint upon the states. The Seventh Circuit agreed with the district court in a 2-1 decision holding that the Second Amendment did not apply to the states.

While the Seventh Circuit was correct in asserting that the Supreme Court has never held that the entire Bill of Rights applied to the states (by being incorporated through the due process clause of the Fourteenth Amendment), the court did not articulate the test by which the Supreme Court determines whether a particular provision is deserving of incorporation. As the dissent in *Quilici* points out, there is an argument that "nothing could be more fundamental to the 'concept of ordered liberty' than the basic right of an individual, within the confines of the criminal law, to protect his home and family from unlawful and dangerous intrusions."

The majority in *Quilici* went further. The court claimed "according to its plain meaning . . . the right to bear arms is inextricably connected to the preservation of a militia" and cited *Miller* for the proposition that "the right to keep and bear arms extends only to those arms which are necessary to maintain a well-regulated militia," ignoring the sentiment that whatever the prelude in the Second Amendment says, the right to keep and bear arms belongs to the people.

The collective rights theory of the Second Amendment, first implicitly rejected in *Miller*, then reanimated in *Tot*, and now advocated by many scholars, is among the most popular theories that seem to ignore the literal meaning of the text of the Second Amendment following the prelude. The collective rights argument proposes that the Second Amendment was primarily intended to prevent federal interference with the militias of the individual states. Since the National Guard has replaced the militias of the individual states, the argument goes, the Second Amendment is little more than an anachronistic curiosity.

The Fourth Circuit in *Love v. Pepersack* concluded that the "lower federal courts have uniformly held that the Second Amendment preserves a collective, rather than individual right" and that it is the "collective right of keeping and bearing arms which must bear a 'reasonable relationship to the preservation or efficiency of a well-regulated militia.'" The defendant in *Pepersack* was found to have failed to identify how her possession of a handgun "will preserve or insure the effectiveness of the militia."

In 1991, former Chief Justice of the United States Warren Burger remarked that firearms advocates' interpretation of the Second Amendment was "the subject of one of the greatest pieces of fraud, I repeat the word 'fraud,' on the American public by special interest groups that I have ever seen in my lifetime. . . . [the NRA has] misled the American people and they, I regret to say, they have had far too much influence on the Congress of the United States than as a citizen I would like to see—and I am a gun man."

Burger also believed that the "very language of the Second Amendment refutes any argument that it was intended to guarantee every citizen an unfettered right to any kind of weapon. . . . [S]urely the Second Amendment does not remotely guarantee

Firearms advocates' interpretation of the Second Amendment, former Chief Justice Warren Burger opined, was "the subject of one of the greatest pieces of fraud . . . on the American public by special interest groups that I have ever seen in my lifetime."

every person the constitutional right to have a 'Saturday Night Special' or a machine gun without any regulation whatever. There is no support in the Constitution for the argument that federal and state governments are powerless to regulate the purchase of such firearms."

The one major exception to the anti-individual-rights trend of Second Amendment jurisprudence is *U.S. v. Emerson*. On March 30, 1999, Sam R.

Cummings, U.S. district judge for Northern Texas, restored a domestic abuser's firearms. Cummings cited the Second Amendment as guaranteeing an individual right to keep and bear arms.

Since the ruling began winding its way through the appeals process, a federal court in *Gillespie v. City of Indianapolis* has ruled that the Second Amendment does not guarantee an individual right to keep and bear arms. If *Emerson* makes it to the Supreme Court, the Second Amendment cases since *Miller* will be reevaluated. It seems likely that an individualist reading of the Second Amendment will someday be upheld by the Supreme Court.

If the Second Amendment is applied to the states or found to contain some individual right, the guns and crime controversy will shift more toward a debate over what the gun control advocates call "the gun problem" and the degree to which a right to bear arms should be regulated.

THE PROBLEM AND THE FIX: HANDGUNS AND GUN LAW

Generally, the gun problem is a handgun problem, not a firearm problem. In the late 1990s, one in four Americans owned at least one firearm, and one in six owned a handgun. About 10 percent of the adult population owned 77 percent of the total stock of civilian-owned firearms, which was estimated at 192 million weapons. A little more than one-third of these 192 million firearms were handguns, but 86 out of every 100 firearm-related crimes involved a handgun. In 1997 there were 89 firearm deaths per day, or a firearm death every 16 minutes, and handguns were used in 79.4 percent of all 1997 firearm homicides.

A Newington, Connecticut, police officer and rescue personnel inspect the bodies of two of four victims a disgruntled worker murdered before turning his gun on himself. The problem of handgun violence has long concerned many Americans—but there is wide disagreement regarding the solution.

The rate of handgun homicides for 1990–1997 was 55.6 percent, indicating a rising trend of handgun involvement in murder, but the statistical peak for handgun homicides occurred in 1993. That year there were 13,258 such killings—out of a total of 16,120 firearm homicides.

As part of an overall drop in 1997, handgun homicides fell to 8,503. Meanwhile, the largest category of firearms fatality is suicide, not homicide. In 1997, 54 percent of all gun deaths were suicides, and 42 percent were homicides. A firearm is used in about 6 of every 10 suicides, and handguns account for an estimated 67 percent of all firearm suicides.

People living in a household with a gun are almost five times more likely to die by suicide than people living in a gun-free home. In addition, suicide is also the leading cause of death among gun buyers in the first year after a gun is purchased, accounting for 25 percent of all deaths, according to a study by Dr. Garen J. Wintemute and colleagues at the University of California at Davis. In the study, deaths among 232,292 people who bought a handgun in California in 1991 were compared with deaths of people in the general population through 1996. The study showed that the first week after a handgun purchase is critical; within that period, the buyer is 57 times more likely than a member of the general population to commit suicide.

Among the 8,503 handgun homicides in 1997, only 193 (2.3 percent) were classified as justifiable homicides by civilians. There were 43 handgun murders for each instance in which a civilian used a handgun to kill in self-defense.

Generally, for every firearm death, there are nearly three gun injuries requiring emergency medical treatment. Conservative estimates place total medical expenses for gunshot injuries in the United States at about $4 billion a year—and that total does not

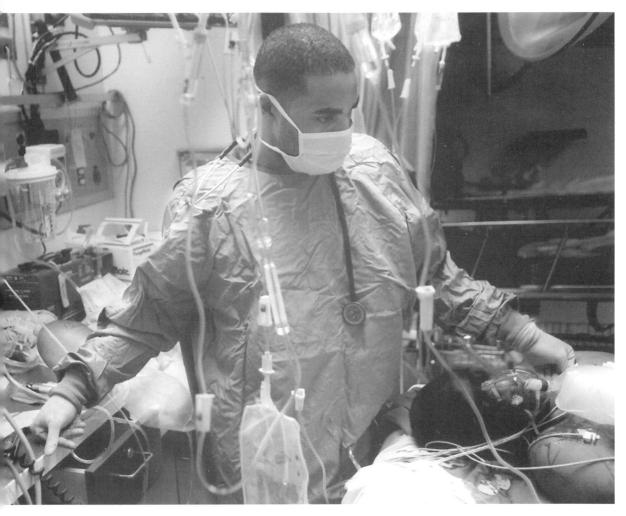

A trauma unit doctor looks at a critically injured patient who has been shot six times in the chest. Each year, gunshot injuries cost an estimated $4 billion in medical expenses alone.

include the cost of lost productivity. In addition, there is the considerable emotional harm that results from gun-related injury, which is impossible to quantify. The suicide of the mother of a student who was severely wounded in the Columbine High School shooting illustrates the potential for a "ripple effect" from violence that cannot be easily accounted for by statistical study.

At the same time, however, gun deaths seem to be on the decline, dropping 21 percent in the period between 1993 and 1997, according to a study released in late 1999. Experts cited as key reasons for this decline a booming economy, better police work, increases in the availability of gun safety courses, and tougher gun laws. Gun laws following the Reagan shooting may deserve significant credit for the reduction in firearms violence.

Before the Brady Act amended federal law, the laws regulating United States firearms traffic included the Gun Control Act of 1968 (GCA), the National Firearms Act (NFA), and the Arms Export Control Act (AECA). The secretary of the Treasury has the authority to administer and enforce these laws, and the secretary has delegated responsibility for enforcing the GCA and NFA, and the import provisions of the AECA, to the Bureau of Alcohol, Tobacco and Firearms (ATF). The authority to enforce the export provisions of the AECA is delegated to the United States Customs Service (USCS).

The GCA was enacted to keep firearms out of the hands of those not legally entitled to possess them because of age, criminal background, or incompetence. The GCA was also designed to make state firearms laws more effective by regulating interstate commerce, channeling firearms sales through federally licensed businesses, and generally confining firearms transactions by nonlicensees to their states of residence.

The NFA regulates certain classes of firearms, including machine guns, short-barrel rifles, short-barrel shotguns, and silencers. The NFA requires that these weapons be registered by their makers, manufacturers, and importers, and imposes taxes on transactions in such weapons.

The AECA gives the president the authority to control imports and exports of "defense articles," including firearms and ammunition, in furtherance of world peace and the security and foreign policy of the United States. The AECA requires permits and licenses to import and export such weapons.

The GCA makes it unlawful to engage in a firearms business without a license. Federal firearms licensees are generally prohibited from transferring firearms to persons who do not reside in the state where the licensee's premises are located. Nonlicensees are generally prohibited from acquiring firearms outside their state of residence or transferring firearms to nonlicensees who reside out of state.

A license is required under the GCA to engage in business as a manufacturer, importer, or dealer in firearms. A license application must include a photograph and fingerprints of the applicant (except in the case of collectors of curios and relics). An application will be approved if the applicant: (1) is 21 years of age or over; (2) is not prohibited from transporting, shipping, or receiving firearms or ammunition in interstate or foreign commerce; (3) has not willfully violated any provision of the GCA; (4) has not willfully failed to disclose any material information or made any false statement; (5) has set up a business premises in a state; and (6) certifies that the business will comply with state and local law and that local law enforcement officials have been notified of the application.

Licenses are issued for a three-year period. Licenses may be revoked, or license renewal applications denied, if the licensee has willfully violated any provision of the GCA.

Judicial review of administrative license denials and revocations may be obtained in federal court. Licensees must maintain records of all firearms receipts and dispositions, including the name, age, and place of residence of each purchaser. Licensed importers and manufacturers are required to identify firearms they import or manufacture by means of a serial number, which must be recorded in licensee

A gun store manager with his wares. Federal law now requires that gun sellers be licensed.

records. Licensees are required to respond immediately to ATF firearms trace requests. Reports of sales to the same individual of two or more handguns at one time or during any five consecutive business days must also be submitted to the ATF. Licensees who discontinue business must deliver their records to the ATF.

These requirements enable ATF to carry out one of the principal purposes of the GCA—assisting state, local, and foreign law enforcement officials in tracing firearms used in crimes. The U.S. government does not maintain records of licensees' firearms transactions except for the control of licensee out-of-business records by the ATF.

The analysis of information from reports of multiple

handgun sales and records of firearms traces provides valuable leads in the identification of illegal gun traffickers and their sources of firearms in the United States. Regulations require that records of all transactions authorized by export, temporary import, and temporary export licenses must be maintained by the licensee for a period of five years. The records must be made available to U.S. Customs officers upon demand. These transactions are also computerized at the Department of State and available to Customs at ports of entry into the United States.

The ATF has a right to conduct inspections, without obtaining warrants, during an annual compliance check, during the course of a criminal investigation of someone other than the licensee, or for purposes of firearms tracing. The ATF may also inspect the records and inventory of licensees by means of an administrative inspection warrant.

The GCA makes it unlawful for certain categories of persons to ship, transport, receive, or possess firearms. Transfers of firearms to any such prohibited persons are also unlawful. These categories include any person: (1) under indictment for a crime punishable by imprisonment for a term exceeding one year; (2) convicted of a crime punishable by imprisonment for a term exceeding one year; (3) who is a fugitive from justice; (4) who is an unlawful user of or addicted to any controlled substance; (5) who is an illegal alien; (6) who has been discharged from the military under dishonorable conditions; (7) who has renounced his or her United States citizenship; (8) who is subject to a court order restraining the person from harassing, stalking, or threatening an intimate partner or child of the intimate partner; or (9) who has been convicted of a misdemeanor crime of domestic violence.

Federal firearms laws prohibit transactions in and possession of certain types of firearms. These include, for example: (1) transfer or possession of a machine gun; (2) manufacture, importation, sale, or possession of any firearm not detectable by airport security devices; (3) manufacture, transfer, or possession of semiautomatic assault weapons; and (4) possession of a firearm not registered as required by the NFA.

Federal firearms laws also include criminal provisions prohibiting certain conduct related to firearms and ammunition. These include, for example: (1) making any false statement or furnishing false identification in acquiring any firearm or ammunition from a licensee; (2) manufacture or importation of armor-piercing ammunition and the sale of such ammunition by manufacturers and importers; (3) theft of firearms; (4) transportation, shipment, possession, or disposal of stolen firearms or ammunition; (5) transportation, shipment, or receipt of firearms having obliterated serial numbers; (6) possession of firearms in a school zone; (7) sale or transfer of a handgun to a juvenile (less than 18 years of age) and possession of a handgun by a juvenile; and (8) use or carrying of a firearm in relation to a crime of violence or drug trafficking crime.

In November of 1993 the Brady Handgun Violence Protection Act (Brady Act) was enacted, amending the GCA. At first, as an interim measure, a waiting period of five days was required "before a licensed importer, manufacturer, or dealer may sell, deliver, or transfer a handgun to an unlicensed individual." The waiting period applied only in states lacking an acceptable alternative system of conducting background checks on handgun purchasers. The interim provisions of the Brady Act became effective on February 28, 1994, and ceased to apply on November 30, 1998, when the permanent provisions of the Brady Law, providing for the establishment of a national instant criminal background check system (NICS) were due to go into effect.

While the interim provisions applied only to handguns, the permanent provisions of the Brady Act apply to all firearms. Permanent provisions of the

Tens of thousands of protesters gathered in Washington, D.C., on May 14, 2000, for the so-called Million Mom March, whose purpose was to demand that Congress pass "common-sense" gun control legislation. Passage of the Brady Act seems to have satisfied neither gun control supporters nor gun rights advocates.

Brady Act require that "with some exceptions, a licensed firearms importer, manufacturer, or dealer [must] contact the national instant criminal background check system (NICS) before transferring any firearm to an unlicensed individual. NICS will advise the licensee whether the system contains any information that the prospective purchaser is prohibited by law from possessing or receiving a firearm." The Brady Act also applies to guns that are loaned or licensed for sport shooting, or to guns that are the subject of pawn recovery.

The act provides that the system may take up to three business days to notify the licensee whether receipt of a firearm by the prospective purchaser would be in violation of law.

Section 922(t) of the Brady Act generally makes it unlawful for any licensed firearms importer, manufacturer, or dealer to sell, deliver, or transfer a firearm to an unlicensed individual (transferee), unless:

1. Before the completion of the transfer, the licensee contacts the national instant background check system.

2. The system provides the licensee with a unique identification number signifying that transfer of the firearm would not be in violation of law, or three business days (meaning a day on which state offices are open) have elapsed from the date the licensee contacted the system and the system has not notified the licensee that receipt of the firearm by the transferee would be in violation of law.

3. The licensee verifies the identity of the transferee by examining a valid identification document containing a photograph of the transferee.

Through June of 1998, the Office of the United States Attorney General estimated that since the passage of the Brady Act, more than 250,000 felons, fugitives, and other prohibited persons had been denied handguns.

Much of the controversy surrounding gun control concerns the various licensing schemes of the states. State laws vary considerably, and one aim of both sides of the gun control debate is to achieve uniformity in the law, for various reasons. Gun rights advocates argue that if you are licensed to carry a concealed weapon in one state, it is wrong to prevent you from exercising your Second Amendment rights in a state that prohibits the carrying of concealed weapons, or in a state that has different licensing standards. Most gun control advocates, on the other hand, generally favor a strict licensing program for gun ownership and for carrying a concealed weapon within a uniform system in which every state has sufficiently high barriers to gun ownership and concealment by criminals or other ineligible persons.

Both sides of the debate have taken positions that tend to suggest some agreement that state laws ought to comport with the Second Amendment in a wholly consistent fashion. Having uniform standards under the Second Amendment of the U.S. Constitution—each state may of course choose separately to have an even stronger statement of rights in the state constitution—is what both sides want. Results from various state licensing schemes following the Brady Act's use tend to indicate that gun violence is dropping as a result of stricter licensing programs, although many gun rights advocates correctly argue that a criminal can still buy handguns at gun shows, from private owners, and on the black market without too much risk of getting caught.

LICENSING SYSTEMS: QUALIFYING FOR THE RIGHT TO BEAR ARMS

As part of the "grand experiment" of constitutional democracy and federalism, state laws regulating certain industries and potentially dangerous articles often differ widely from one another. For example, as of 1999, Vermont was the only state where the carrying of a concealed weapon was lawful without a license.

At the same time, carrying a concealed weapon was prohibited in Illinois, Kansas, Missouri, Nebraska, New Mexico, Ohio, and Wisconsin. In another 14 states, the carrying of a concealed weapon required a license issued by police, who are permitted to approve or deny an application based on an applicant's full record. In another 29 states, almost every nonfelon can acquire a license to carry a concealed weapon, or CCW license.

In the states where the police examine the applicant's full record with discretion to deny the CCW license based upon things other than felony convictions, the licensing program is called "may-issue licensing."

97

This is in contrast to the "shall-issue" licensing policies of states denying CCW licenses only to applicants with prior convictions of certain serious criminal offenses.

May-issue licensing additionally requires that the applicant demonstrate a specific need to carry a concealed weapon. A merchant whose business requires the regular transport of a large amount of money to a bank would be an example of an applicant with such a need. A may-issue license also usually restricts the gun owner to carrying a weapon only at certain times and places. CCW licenses are infrequently issued in most of these may-issue states: Alabama, California, Delaware, Georgia, Hawaii, Iowa, Maryland, Massachusetts, Michigan, Minnesota, New Jersey, New York, Rhode Island, and South Carolina.

In most of the shall-issue states—Alaska, Arizona, Arkansas, Colorado, Connecticut, Florida, Idaho, Indiana, Kentucky, Louisiana, Maine, Mississippi, Montana, Nevada, New Hampshire, North Carolina, North Dakota, Oklahoma, Oregon, Pennsylvania, South Carolina, South Dakota, Tennessee, Texas, Utah, Virginia, Washington, West Virginia, and Wyoming—applicants are not required to demonstrate need to be granted a license. In addition, in most of these states, applicants can obtain a license by merely claiming a lawful purpose such as basic self-defense, unrestricted to particular times and locations. Among the shall-issue states, however, Colorado in particular does not require a showing of need, but law enforcement officials there have considerable discretion in granting a CCW permit, rendering it difficult in practice to obtain CCW licensure in Colorado as of 1997.

Shall-issue licensing systems generally require the applicant to meet certain criteria. To receive a license to carry a concealed weapon in public, the person in most shall-issue states must at minimum: (1) be at least 21 years of age; (2) be a resident of the state; (3) provide fingerprints; (4) submit to a criminal and mental

Supporters of granting licenses for the carrying of concealed weapons say that such arrangements deter would-be criminals and offer citizens the best odds for self-defense.

health background check; (5) have not been convicted of a felony or any crime punishable by imprisonment for more than one year; (6) not be a fugitive from justice; (7) not be an illegal alien; (8) not be an unlawful user of or be addicted to any controlled substance; (9) not have been adjudicated mentally incompetent or been committed to a mental institution; (10) not have been dishonorably discharged from any branch of the U.S. military; (11) not be subject to a restraining or protection order; (12) not have been convicted of a misdemeanor crime of domestic violence; (13) not be awaiting trial for, and not have any charges pending for, a crime punishable by more than one year's imprisonment; (14) have completed a firearms safety or training course; and (15) pay a licensing fee.

The term of the license varies from two to five years. A four-year term is most common. Fees to acquire a permit, not including training course costs and finger-printing fees, which several states assess separately, vary from a few dollars to more than $135.

Gun rights supporters arguing for a universal CCW shall-issue licensing system point out that, according to Department of Justice statistics, approximately 87 percent of violent crime occurs outside the home. The supporters emphasize that, despite the fact that Americans possess approximately 70 million handguns, one is not armed if one does not have a weapon at hand when needed.

The gun rights lobby argues that may-issue licensing laws and prohibitions against the carrying of weapons succeed only in disarming those who respect the law, and that, perversely, by ensuring that those who abide by the law will not carry weapons outside the home, may-issue licensing laws aid and abet criminals by assuring them that they will find unarmed, easy victims. The gun rights lobby also argues that shall-issue concealed-carry laws, by contrast, deprive criminals of peace of mind, and are based upon a right of self-defense.

It is true that every state recognizes a right of its citizens to use lethal force in self-defense in certain situations. As many commentators suggest, such self-defense is not lawlessness but in accord with the law and in accord with the same law the police rely on in deciding when to use lethal force.

Gun rights advocates often claim that the right to self-defense belongs to each person, not merely those who the police or other licensing authorities believe deserve to have that right. However, this argument ignores the need for reasonable control over gun licensing because not everyone has a right to self-defense—or at least not everyone enjoys that right to the same degree. Criminals and other people ineligible to obtain a gun permit may retain their right of self-defense, but in a fashion that does not protect them from criminal punishment should they violate a gun law even in a legitimate self-defense situation. One of the basic features of any criminal justice system is that certain rights are lost by those proven to have violated certain rules of behavior—behavior that has been defined as criminal. Any right of self-defense relating to the Second Amendment is lost when a person goes to jail. No inmate can claim a right of self-defense against the prison authority or the government (and unfortunately not against fellow inmates either), and other ineligible but not incarcerated persons face the same loss of Second Amendment rights. Even a fundamental constitutional right has limits, and usually those limits are found by looking at conflicting rights.

Shall-issue supporters cite studies by John Lott of the University of Chicago, revealing that murder rates dropped by 8.5 percent and rapes by 5 percent in states that allowed citizens to carry concealed firearms. These statistics, shall-issue proponents say, bolster the argument that residents of states that permit concealed weapons ought to have the right to protect themselves with a gun when they travel to states that bar concealed weapons.

According to New York attorney and author Jeffrey R. Snyder, arguments opposing the adoption of shall-issue licensing systems generally fall into seven categories: (1) "the police know best" argument for retaining discretionary systems; (2) police officer safety; (3) the potential danger to the citizen from carrying a firearm; (4) the inability of ordinary citizens to successfully defend themselves with a firearm; (5) the inadequacy of firearms for self-defense; (6) the general threats to public safety resulting from firearms; and (7) the most common and basic argument, best summed up by the phrase "the blood will run in the streets." These arguments are the subject of considerable debate between the gun control lobby and firearms-rights advocates.

A police officer in Philadelphia visits the spot where a fellow officer was shot to death. Most police officers don't seem to favor concealed-weapons licenses, believing that the presence of handguns on the streets makes policing more dangerous.

The "police know best" argument is used by opponents of concealed-carry laws to argue for the retention of discretionary systems. Police, the argument goes, are uniquely qualified because of the nature of their work and their experience, and have the best idea of whom to trust with a gun license among the persons they serve in any given community. Overriding such judgment is risky, or so this argument goes, because trusting experience is usually better than imposing rigid, objective standards permitting practically any law-abiding citizen to carry a gun. This argument may ignore whatever right the Second Amendment provides to "keep and bear Arms" in the context of self-defense, and it empowers the licensing authority (the police) to use broad and unchecked discretion, which usually means an overly high incidence of abuse.

More than 60 years of discretionary licensing laws in America have apparently demonstrated that the determination of who deserves or needs to carry a gun is not consistently or often rationally or fairly made under discretionary licensing programs.

Discretionary licensing, Snyder points out, is supported by an argument for a government by men, not by laws—something quite at odds with the Framers' intent during the drafting of the Constitution.

However, many if not most law enforcement officials believe that an armed citizenry makes police work more dangerous while failing to achieve one important aim of handgun legislation: keeping guns away from criminals who have not yet been convicted of a crime. Police officer discretion as allowed in may-issue licensing jurisdictions might offer the only opportunity for denial of a weapon based on the rap sheet or history of an individual that is less than clean but without felony conviction.

Without the use of such discretion, it seems likely that the "wrong" people will have the same level of easy access to gun permits as people with no criminal history and no history of personal problems that might indicate some need for further analysis. For example, Floridians not formally declared guilty as part of a plea bargain, but charged with crimes such as battery, aggravated battery, auto theft, trespassing, shoplifting, or prowling were able to obtain CCW licenses after Florida weakened its CCW law. The gunman who murdered seven fellow Xerox employees in Hawaii in 1999 had a short rap sheet involving a criminal damaging charge. Although denying a potential murderer a permit is not the same as denying that person access to a gun, the fact remains that a discretionary system of licensing and selling handguns might prevent violence in instances where the potential murderer is delayed in obtaining a weapon and the delay causes time to pass and the disturbed person's emotions to cool. The opposite argument is that laws and licensing procedures mean little or nothing to

A prosecutor holds the gun Byran Uyesugi used to murder seven coworkers at a Xerox office in Hawaii in 1999. Uyesugi had a rap sheet but not a felony record that would have barred him from getting a gun permit.

people who are mentally deranged or not concerned with following laws.

While legitimate privacy concerns arise when considering whether to allow the police to review medical or mental health records before issuing a gun permit, a strong argument can be made for the need to protect society from "unbalanced" or emotionally damaged or neurologically impaired individuals. The need for protection may slightly outweigh any presumptive right of personal self-defense or personal privacy in the issuance of gun licenses.

The argument that the carrying of handguns by law-abiding citizens jeopardizes the safety of the police by increasing the risk that they will be shot—either by hot-headed, previously law-abiding citizens or in shoot-outs involving previously law-abiding citizens now taking the law into their own hands—is not supported by experience. Licensed, law-abiding gun owners have so far not used their guns to assault police officers who stop them for traffic violations or other minor infractions. The argument presumes that the act of carrying a gun is synonymous with intent to take the law into one's own hands.

Nevertheless, police are trained how to judge situations under extreme duress and how to properly handle the speed and complexity of unfolding confrontations. Private citizens are not. Even if most citizens with CCW permits will never be tempted to use their guns unwisely, the potential for more violence is probably increased by shall-issue licensing schemes.

The argument that guns are far more dangerous as instrumentalities, in their own right, focuses upon the connection between gun availability and gun use: that by having a gun one is more likely to accidentally shoot someone, or impulsively use the gun to commit suicide, or use the gun during an otherwise routine interpersonal dispute, such as during an episode of road rage.

An article in the *New England Journal of Medicine* contained a study that showed that a gun in the home is 43 times more likely to be used in a suicide, criminal homicide, or accidental gunshot death than to kill in self-protection. Arguing by analogy, opponents of concealed weapon permits use the study to claim that if the gun is so dangerous in the home, it will be unacceptably dangerous in public. Another aspect of the argument is the implication that the greater peace of mind supposedly gained from walking the streets armed is probably outweighed by actual safety risks from sources other than criminal attack.

Serious problems with the study's assumptions exist. The study measures the benefits of gun ownership only in terms of a "body count" of criminals killed by gun-toting citizens. It ignores the real deterrent effect of brandishing a firearm when confronted by a potential assailant.

Criminologist Gary Kleck found that more than 75 percent of the time firearms are used defensively they are not actually fired. As attorney Jeffrey R. Snyder points out, measuring the social benefits of firearm ownership by body count is "no less misguided than measuring the benefits of the police solely by the number of criminals they kill each year." Another problem with the study is that more than half of the deaths recorded on the gun-ownership side were suicides. The presupposition is that none of these people would have committed suicide if they did not have a gun at the moment they decided to commit suicide, which at best seems unlikely.

Because a large number of homicide victims just happen to be criminals, and because criminals are often armed, the study's analysis is undermined further. The focus on household homicide sites may have yielded information only about specific groups of people (such as the victims or people who commit murder), and this information may not be reliable enough to allow generalization to the entire adult population. As Snyder observed:

> It is possible that the households in which homicides occur are far from representative of typical or average households in which guns are present. If so, treating the 43 times statistic as though it were a universal law applicable to all gun owners, rather than as descriptive of a discrete, aberrant subset, is simply wrong and misleading. Thus, while it is tautologically true that one cannot have an accident with a gun, commit suicide with a gun, or kill a loved one or friend in a moment of anger with a gun unless one first has a gun, there is no good evidence to support claims that those possibilities are more likely and prevalent occurrences for the typical gun owner— and a greater risk to the typical gun owner or his family members—than are the potential benefits of gun ownership.

Nevertheless, having a gun in the home does present some degree of risk that is not present when there is no gun in the household. Many objections to concealed-carry licensure relate to the inadequacy of training requirements. Although gun safety training is an important aspect of gun ownership, there are no statistically significant relationships between the number of hours of gun safety training and the actual harm caused by gun owners. Generally, citizens who obtain concealed-carry permits understand that unless they are clearly threatened in a situation where armed self-defense is the only option, shooting someone will result in enormous legal difficulties.

Even if 8 to 16 hours of training is too little to turn the neophyte gun owner into a professional marksman and gun-safety expert, more training is probably a better antidote to the problem than a prohibition of concealed weapons. While it is good to be wary of the false confidence and insufficient skill level of a new gun owner, there is no reliable proof that such factors outweigh the actual preventive effect of having a citizenry's potential firepower feared by criminals. Nor has the actual experience with concealed-carry permits yielded any cause for alarm over the issue of how well prepared a permit-holder is to actually use the weapon in a responsible manner.

Because a citizen under attack by a criminal is likely to be in a very unambiguous situation, the level of training needed to deal with the attack is probably very minimal. While it would be dangerous to shoot at a criminal in a crowded public area, for example, most criminal attacks on private citizens do not take place in an area filled with bystanders.

Police, trained much more extensively than concealed-carry permit holders, actually kill more innocent bystanders than private citizens engaged in acts of self-defense. Of course, police are much more likely than private citizens to encounter situations that require the use of deadly force. Police frequently deal with situations involving a high level of ambiguity and angry, cornered, or fleeing criminal suspects. Most police officers killed in the line of duty do not fire at their killer. For example, an FBI study of 51 incidents in which 54 police officers died in the line of duty showed that 85 percent of the time the officer did not fire his or her gun. On the other hand, concealed-carry permit holders probably encounter less ambiguity when faced with a criminal attack, making the gun-safety-training issue largely irrelevant.

The "why bother?" argument is that people should not want to carry a gun because of the comparative rarity of instances in which a citizen actually confronts a criminal attack. Although studies show varying instances of gun use in self-defense, ranging from 65,000 to more than 3 million times per year, the "why bother?" argument may miss an important point. Having a smoke alarm in the event of a fire, and a first-aid kit in the event of an emergency, are not examples of behaviors that are unwise because of the low probability of the risk.

Opponents of gun control also argue that one might not be able to get to the weapon in time, or that sometimes the best course of action when confronted by an armed robber is to do nothing to provoke attack, or that even if armed there is no guarantee that one will not be killed by the assailant anyway. These aspects of the same argument fail for the same reason. It is not the probability of success that dictates the wisdom of preventive action, but the personal decision to take measures to ensure against worse problems in the event that a rare or emergency situation occurs. As Snyder argues, "If the fear is that people will not recognize firearms' limitations or will try to use guns inappropriately, the answer is education, not prohibition."

National Institute of Justice statistics show that persons who resist crime with a firearm are less likely to be injured, or are likely to be injured less severely, than persons who either cooperate with their assailants or resist by some means other than a firearm. Remarkably, even if the assailant is armed with a gun, the odds of the victim escaping serious injury remain higher when the victim can respond with at least a show of armed force. While opponents of concealed-carry laws dispute the notion that ordinary citizens can successfully defend themselves, the statistical evidence so far shows that a victim's deployment of a firearm enhances the victim's chances for survival and reduces his or her chances for serious injury.

The simplistic, linear argument that more guns cause more violence simply advances the idea that the more guns present in society (on the street), the more harm that must come from gun use. While such a notion might prove true in the case of land mines placed where people must walk, experience shows that more handguns do not necessarily lead to more death and injury. For example, in 1973 there were an estimated 122 million firearms and 36.9 million handguns, and the homicide rate was 9.4 per 100,000 people. Twenty years later, at the end of 1992, there were 221.9 million firearms, 77.6 million handguns, and a lower homicide rate (8.5 percent).

Snyder makes the point that what is important is not the number of guns but the people using them. The available evidence indicates that firearms in the hands of permit holders are not a law enforcement problem and are not a source of social harm—with rare exception. A better argument, according to Snyder, can be made concerning the measure of social utility versus social harm of having so many guns:

> A more sophisticated approach is to build a general case that the total social harm related to firearms far outweighs any social benefits associated with their ownership and use. The numbers tell a decidedly grim story: in 1994, for example, there were approximately 1.3 million gun crimes. A few more than 22,000 people were murdered with

Gun rights advocates say that more handguns doesn't necessarily mean more death and injury. But for gun control supporters, the connection seems clear.

firearms, an approximately equal number committed suicide with firearms, and about 100,000 people were treated in hospitals or emergency rooms for nonfatal gunshot wounds (including self-inflicted wounds from suicide attempts and accidents). On the other hand, firearms are used defensively (it is argued) only about 65,000 to 80,000 times a year. The result is that the societal costs associated with firearm misuse far exceed the societal benefits from their use.

Recently, however, the debate over whether violence is in fact increasing as a result of the increase in handgun ownership is giving way to concerns regarding the dangers of handguns in the home and the high percentage of handgun involvement in crime. Of course, such arguments do not answer the question of whether an individual's right of self-defense constitutionally trumps social cost-benefit calculations.

"Blood will run in the streets"—Snyder calls this "the most powerful rhetorical argument that is generally made by those who oppose shall-issue licensing laws." So far, American streets since 1987 have not been turned into "Dodge City" or any reasonable facsimile of the lawless mythical "Wild West." Given experience so far and the stringent licensing requirements, there appears to be little reason not to trust citizens who earn such permits, nor is there any strong reason to believe that carrying a gun, by itself, is enough to transform an otherwise law-abiding person into an irresponsible shooter.

So far, results from concealed-carry "shall-license" states show that the number of persons currently in possession of permits to carry firearms ranges from 1 to 5 percent of the state's population; that criminals do not apply for permits; and that large numbers of permit holders do not take to settling their traffic disputes or arguments with guns, or otherwise "take the law into their own hands." Shall-issue licensing states have almost no problems with violent criminality or inappropriate brandishing of firearms by permit holders, and some permit holders have used their guns to defend themselves and others.

Ultimately, the question of whether gun control reduces crime or merely allows criminals more peace of mind in approaching an unarmed citizenry is beside the point. Just as the Second Amendment right to bear arms against potential government tyranny is not a right that depends on a genuine, immediate, identifiable threat from a government, so too does the right to prepare reasonable means of self-protection not require the apprehension of immediate danger.

21ST-CENTURY GUNS: THE FUTURE OF THE SECOND AMENDMENT

A scientist working on the "smart gun" project at Sandia National Laboratories in Albuquerque, New Mexico, holds a prototype. A computer chip would enable the gun to "recognize" its owner and prevent anyone else from firing the weapon. In the future, technology may help solve some of the problems associated with handguns.

At the beginning of the 21st century, dramatic changes in the very terms of the gun debate may be on the horizon. If such changes do in fact occur, the courts will likely play a key role—but not through criminal cases and appeals that require further examination and clarification of the meaning of the Second Amendment. Rather, such change may well come from civil cases—namely, product liability lawsuits filed against gun manufacturers.

Following the model of litigation that led to a multi-billion-dollar settlement from tobacco companies, a group of America's most powerful trial lawyers is poised to take on the nation's gun manufacturers. By filing lawsuits against these manufacturers under product liability or negligence laws—essentially holding gun manufacturers financially responsible for accidental and criminal gunshot deaths and injuries—the trial lawyers may succeed in creating a kind of de facto gun control far more restrictive than Congress has been willing to enact.

Several American city and county governments began suing gun makers in 1999. Ironically, many of these localities—including Boston, Detroit, and Alameda County, California—brought legal actions while conducting firearms distribution, usually through police-force-run "swaps" of guns.

A gun swap is a way to defray the cost of purchasing new police weapons. Around the time of its lawsuit, Boston sold more than 3,000 police-issue .38-caliber handguns while proposing a new legal theory that gun sellers should be held liable when those sellers display a "willful blindness" to what happens to the guns after the sale.

The mayor of New Orleans, the first city to sue gun manufacturers, recently announced his city's intent to get guns off the streets. New Orleans, with one of the highest murder rates of all American cities, was preparing to sue gun manufacturers while at the same time using an Indiana broker to put more than 7,000 guns, including the particularly lethal TEC-9s and various other semiautomatics whose importation and manufacture Congress banned in 1994, back on the streets.

The lawsuits are based upon a legal argument deeming it unconscionable for manufacturers to fill the demand of shops in gun-friendly states if they can reasonably expect that a certain percentage of their merchandise will wind up on city streets in cities with gun prohibition. Ironically, guns that New Orleans regularly shipped to Texas soon made it back for sale in New Orleans gun shops, making the New Orleans suit against gun manufacturers rather curious indeed.

Gun litigation began after the success of similar lawsuits against the tobacco industry. After meeting in Chicago in December 1998, a group of America's richest trial lawyers began offering their services to various municipalities, mayors, and city attorneys, proposing to work on contingency fees that in some instances approached 30 percent of any trial winnings. The pending suits comprise a uniquely American way of creating new theories of liability, and promise to involve the courts in Second Amendment analysis if the suits are not dismissed.

In response to the "sue the manufacturers" movement, gun-rights activists—including the Second Amendment Foundation, based in Bellevue, Washington—recently sued the U.S. Conference of Mayors, alleging a conspiracy to violate the rights of gun owners by encouraging cities and city mayors to sue firearms manufacturers. Lawsuits may be filed individually against the more than 20 mayors whose cities have filed suit against gun manufacturers.

Although gun manufacturers will defend against product-liability and other such lawsuits without utilizing the Second Amendment, there will likely be some argument that in fact the Second Amendment has some relevance to the arms manufacturing industry. However, the plaintiff lawyers are not necessarily trying to take the question of gun manufacturer liability to court. Instead, many commentators believe, their ultimate aim is to convince the manufacturers to agree to a large settlement, as happened with the tobacco companies.

Peter J. Boyer, in a May 19, 1999, *New Yorker* article published before more than 20 cities filed such suits, observed: "If twenty cities do bring suits, defending against them, according to some estimates, could cost the gun manufacturers as much as a million dollars a day." That would force gun makers to the negotiating table as the only alternative to bankruptcy. Although some of the lawsuits filed by cities have already been dismissed, more continue to be filed and upheld against motions to dismiss.

In December 1999, a judge in Chicago refused to grant dismissal and ruled that it was "clear to this court" that gun companies knowingly violated Chicago's strict antihandgun laws by oversupplying gun shops in the suburbs, where the laws are weaker, thus "creating an underground market."

On the federal side, according to the *National Law Journal*, the NAACP was trying to get its new suit against gun makers heard by Brooklyn judge Jack Weinstein, because the underlying theories "might not succeed in any other courtroom in America." Weinstein presided over *Hamilton v. Accu-Tek*, the first case in which a jury bought the idea of holding manufacturers responsible for gun violence because they should have known that some of their products would end up in the hands of criminals. The jurors did not accept this theory easily. During six days of deliberations, they repeatedly told Judge Weinstein that they could not reach agreement. He refused to accept a deadlock. Such decisions may well be reversed on appeal, but the trial lawyers' apparent aim is to create as much uncertainty as possible, capitalizing on the difficulty of defending against many different theories in many different places at once.

"[We] have the resources to start a war instead of taking little potshots," trial lawyer John Coale told the *New Yorker*'s Boyer. "Well, we've started a war." Attorney Dennis Henigan of the Center to Prevent Handgun Violence revealed that he seeks to create a "credible threat of liability." According to Henigan, the "more cities that file, the greater is the threat. So what you really want is a diversity of cases in lots of different regions, lots of different courts to create the greatest threat of liability."

Polls show that gun suits are unpopular even among voters who are willing to entertain other gun control proposals. Whether the press will turn critical is a good question. The *New Yorker*'s account depicts attorney Coale openly gloating over the success of the tobacco lawyers in getting the media to play along. "With Coale directing the political and media ends of the case," as Boyer tells it, "the plaintiffs' lawyers became the prime creators and marketers of a national narrative entitled 'Big Tobacco.'"

U.S. District Court judge Jack Weinstein is considered amenable to the notion that gun manufacturers can be sued under product liability and negligence laws.

According to Boyer, the "most important lessons" Henigan brought to the group of trial lawyers for whom Coale became a spokesman "had nothing to do with litigation" but instead related to manipulating public opinion. "Henigan believes that it is imperative to steer the argument about guns away from the problematic area of criminal use, with its inconvenient focus on criminals" and instead recast the gun debate "as a health issue . . . guns should be thought of as pathogens, and gun ownership, perhaps, as a disease."

Boyer concluded that, given their power to decide which suits to file next and how to prosecute them, "Coale and his colleagues are guiding the national agenda—a new means of public-policy making that can't be found in any civics book." The reason it can't be found in any civics book is because it is not the form of government the Founders thought they were designing in the Constitution. The June 1999 *American Lawyer*, in its article recounting the origins of the firearms litigation, reports that prominent New Orleans trial lawyer Wendell Gauthier was the first to talk his colleagues into suing gun makers, even though their pockets weren't all that deep. The suit "fit with Gauthier's notion of the plaintiffs bar as a de facto fourth branch of government, one that achieved regulation through litigation where legislation failed."

It was the trial lawyers themselves who called themselves a de facto fourth branch of government. "That's their view of the matter," according to the *American Lawyer*. The controversy around the trial lawyers' ethics and power is sure to continue even as more lawsuits are filed. Since those who labor in the other three branches of government aren't supposed to use their powers to turn themselves into billionaires without having to submit to the voters or to public scrutiny—including sunshine laws, extensive financial disclosures and blind trusts, and freedom of information laws—it may only be fair for legislators to try to suppress the "legislation by settlement extortion" movement.

The pressure of gun litigation is beginning to show. A gun dealer agreed to stop selling handguns and pay $10,000 to get itself dropped from the lawsuit filed by Gary, Indiana, one of the nation's most violent cities, which for three years in the 1990s was the city with the highest murder rate per capita. The Gary lawsuit accused the gun industry of putting weapons into criminals' hands.

Aside from the litigation against gun manufacturers,

Bob Baker talks with a worker at Freedom Arms, his family's business. Baker claims that product liability lawsuits have cost him more than $200,000 and forced him to lay off 12 of his 35 employees.

the 21st century will feature technology that will either prevent more criminals from obtaining weapons or make weapons safer. Recently, federal and local law enforcement officials began using a new nationwide computer system that aims to trace guns used during crimes. The system, called Online Lead, is administered by the Treasury Department's Bureau of Alcohol, Tobacco and Firearms.

"Online Lead takes our fight against gun traffickers into cyberspace," said Treasury secretary Lawrence Summers, observing that the technology "gives federal, state and local law enforcement officials throughout the country a new tool to help identify and arrest gun traffickers."

The system is in use at all 331 ATF field offices. Police and other local law enforcement officials access the system through the ATF computer network. Law enforcement officials are not required to ask ATF to trace guns used during crimes but are encouraged to do so, and the results are entered into a national database. By the end of 1999 that database had information on more than 1 million traced firearms. ATF has been tracing guns used in crimes for years, but the new software should make it much easier for investigators to analyze trends and patterns in illegal firearms trafficking. The system evolved from earlier projects that stored information on traced guns on computer disks that had to be shipped to ATF field offices.

Agents start with a gun's make and serial number, moving from the manufacturer to a wholesaler and distributor to the first retail sale by a federally licensed gun dealer.

Sales by individuals or by collectors at gun shows are still considered private and exempt from such record-keeping requirements. Gun control supporters want to strengthen gun laws by requiring background checks on gun-show weapon sales, banning violent juvenile offenders from owning guns when they turn 21, requiring child safety locks to be sold with handguns, and banning the import of high-capacity ammunition clips. Gun rights advocates will continue to try to make the Second Amendment a limit on such legislation. Meanwhile, new technology may offer options agreeable to both sides of the gun rights debate.

If a so-called smart gun technology—which allows a gun to be fired only by its owner and only in a direction away from the owner—became commercially available, many of the problems of accidental gun violence would be solved if the guns replaced all the "nonsmart" guns in private ownership. It is hoped by nearly everyone on both sides of the gun debate that when some future John Hinckley points a gun at a president, the gun will be a "super-smart" gun—able to recognize that the shooter intends to use the gun illegally. If advances in technology bring us to a "super-smart" gun era, an understanding of the Second Amendment may have to be an integral part of the "super-smart" gun's "intelligence" to produce a good definition of illegal use. But such a scenario seems far in the future. Early in the 21st century the gun debate promises to be in the news on an almost daily basis until a case leads the Supreme Court to issue a more definitive account of the precise nature and applicability of the Second Amendment right to keep and bear arms.

Further Reading

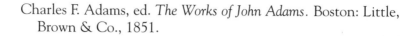

Charles F. Adams, ed. *The Works of John Adams*. Boston: Little, Brown & Co., 1851.

Ansell, S. T. "Legal and Historical Aspects of the Militia," 26 *Yale Law Journal*, 471–480, 1917.

Bailyn, Bernard. *The Ideological Origins of the American Revolution*. Cambridge, Mass.: The Belknap Press of Harvard University Press, 1967.

Blackstone, William. *Commentaries on the Laws of England*. Chicago: University of Chicago Press, 1979.

Boorstin, Daniel J. *The Colonial Experience*. New York: Random House, 1958.

Burgh, James. *2 Political Disquisitions: or An Enquiry Into Public Errors, Defects, and Abuses*. London, 1774–75. Chicago: University of Chicago Press.

Denning, Brannon P. "Can the Simple Cite be Trusted?: Lower Court Interpretations of *United States v. Miller* and the Second Amendment." 26 *Cumberland Law Review*, 961–1004, 1996.

Dowlut, Robert. "The Right to Keep and Bear Arms: A Right to Self-Defense Against Criminals and Despots." 8 *Stanford Law & Policy Review*, 25–40, 1997.

Gray, Vernon. "Civil Disobedience." *St. Mary's Today*, May 28, 1996, 39.

Levinson, Sanford. "The Embarrassing Second Amendment." 99 *Yale Law Journal*, 637–659, 1989.

Mullins, Patrick Todd. "The Militia Clauses, the National Guard, and Federalism: A Constitutional Tug of War." 57 *George Washington Law Review*, 328, 1988.

Further Reading

Story, Joseph. *Commentary on the Constitution*. Boston: Hilliard, Gray, 1833.

Thorpe, Francis N. *The Federal and State Constitutions, Colonial Charters, and Other Organic Laws*. Washington, D.C.: Government Printing Office, 1909.

Tucker, Henry St. George. *Commentaries on the Laws of Virginia* 43. Richmond, Va.: Shepard and Colin, 1846.

Weatherup, Roy G. "Standing Armies and Armed Citizens: An Historical Analysis of the Second Amendment." 2 *Hastings Constitutional Law Quarterly*, 961–1001, 1975.

Young, David, ed. *The Origin of the Second Amendment: A Documentary History of the Bill of Rights 1787–1792*. Golden Oaks Books, 1995.

Index

Index

126

JUSTIN FERNANDEZ is a licensed attorney in Ohio, a former law clerk for the Ohio Court of Appeals, Second Appellate District, and the author of *High Crimes and Misdemeanors: The Impeachment Process* (Chelsea House, 2000).

AUSTIN SARAT is William Nelson Cromwell Professor of Jurisprudence and Political Science at Amherst College, where he also chairs the Department of Law, Jurisprudence and Social Thought. Professor Sarat is the author or editor of 23 books and numerous scholarly articles. Among his books are *Law's Violence, Sitting in Judgment: Sentencing the White Collar Criminal,* and *Justice and Injustice in Law and Legal Theory.* He has received many academic awards and held several prestigious fellowships. He is President of the Law & Society Association and Chair of the Working Group on Law, Culture and the Humanities. In addition, he is a nationally recognized teacher and educator whose teaching has been featured in the *New York Times,* on the *Today* show, and on National Public Radio's *Fresh Air.*

Picture Credits